Teaching Healthy Lifestyles in Middle School PE

Strategies From an Award-Winning Program

Crystal Gorwitz

NASPE National Middle School Physical Education
Teacher of the Year, 2004

NASPE STARS School Award Winner, 2005 and 2008

Human Kinetics

Library of Congress Cataloging-in-Publication Data

Gorwitz, Crystal.
 Teaching healthy lifestyles in middle school PE : strategies from an award-winning program / Crystal Gorwitz.
     p. cm.
  Includes index.
  ISBN-13: 978-0-7360-8678-3 (soft cover)
  ISBN-10: 0-7360-8678-1 (soft cover)
  1. Physical education and training--Study and teaching (Middle school)--United States. 2. Physical education and training--Curricula--United States. 3. Health education--Study and teaching (Middle School)--United States. I. Title.
  GV365.G67 2012
  613.7071'2--dc23

                         2011025489

ISBN-10: 0-7360-8678-1 (print)
ISBN-13: 978-0-7360-8678-3 (print)

The web addresses cited in this text were current as of April 2011, unless otherwise noted.

Acquisitions Editor: Scott Wikgren; **Developmental Editor:** Jacqueline Eaton Blakley; **Assistant Editor:** Anne Rumery; **Copyeditor:** Tom Tiller; **Indexer:** Sharon Duffy; **Permissions Manager:** Dalene Reeder; **Graphic Designer and Cover Designer:** Robert Reuther; **Graphic Artist:** Dawn Sills; **Photographer (cover):** Courtesy of Crystal Gorwitz; **Photographer (interior):** Courtesy of Crystal Gorwitz, unless otherwise noted; **Art Manager:** Kelly Hendren; **Associate Art Manager:** Alan L. Wilborn; **Printer:** United Graphics

Printed in the United States of America   10   9   8   7   6   5   4   3   2   1

The paper in this book is certified under a sustainable forestry program.

Human Kinetics
Website: www.HumanKinetics.com

United States: Human Kinetics
P.O. Box 5076
Champaign, IL 61825-5076
800-747-4457
e-mail: humank@hkusa.com

Canada: Human Kinetics
475 Devonshire Road Unit 100
Windsor, ON N8Y 2L5
800-465-7301 (in Canada only)
e-mail: info@hkcanada.com

Europe: Human Kinetics
107 Bradford Road
Stanningley
Leeds LS28 6AT, United Kingdom
+44 (0) 113 255 5665
e-mail: hk@hkeurope.com

Australia: Human Kinetics
57A Price Avenue
Lower Mitcham, South Australia 5062
08 8372 0999
e-mail: info@hkaustralia.com

New Zealand: Human Kinetics
P.O. Box 80
Torrens Park, South Australia 5062
0800 222 062
e-mail: info@hknewzealand.com

E4943

Contents

Preface

What if I told you that your teaching can make a positive difference for your students today and every day for the rest of their lives? You probably already believe this, or you would never have gone into teaching in the first place! But any of us can get worn down by the grind of our daily work, by job requirements that seem to have little to do with our students' needs, by the perceived lack of success and advancement of our students. Unfortunately, many of us eventually find ourselves discouraged, wondering whether our efforts are really helping the kids we care for, searching in vain for the passion that once inspired our work.

But I'm here to assure you that with small steps, big changes can happen in your program! Your vision for your students is the key that will help you forge a PATH to their success! I will share with you how I have built a middle school physical education program in which students learn what choices they need to make in order to live a healthy lifestyle and are empowered to make those choices. (The principles can be applied to other K-12 levels as well.) The program's quality has been recognized in the following ways:

- In 2001, our district (Hortonville School District, Hortonville, Wisconsin) was awarded a Carol M. White Physical Education Program (PEP) grant in the amount of $233,604. (You can go to www2.ed.gov/programs/ whitephysed/index.html to read more about this program.) PEP grants are awarded to schools and organizations that seek to initiate, expand, or enhance physical education programs for K-12 students. Grant recipients must implement programs that help students make progress toward meeting state standards. The Hortonville physical education teachers (elementary, middle school, and high school) teamed up to identify weaknesses in our program and write a proposal for addressing those weaknesses. Our proposal earned us a grant from this very competitive program to fund our vision! (More on how we went about this process in chapter 1.)

- Twice (in 2005 and 2008) our school has been selected as a NASPE STARS school. "Through the STARS self-study and review process, NASPE identifies and honors physical education programs that model the essential elements for high-quality physical education and provide meaningful learning opportunities for all students. STARS schools exemplify excellence in teaching students the knowledge, skills, and confidence needed for motor development to achieve movement competency and health-related fitness and promote lifelong physical activity" (www.aahperd.org/naspe/awards/recognitionPrograms/STARS/about.cfm).

■ In 2004 I had the honor of being named NASPE National Middle School Physical Education Teacher of the Year. Although this is an individual award, I never could have achieved it without years of collaboration and cooperation with countless colleagues!

Why has Hortonville received this kind of recognition? You could chalk it up to dedicated teachers, supportive administrators, maybe a little luck. . . . But more than anything, the recognition has come from *results*! Kids in our district enjoy physical education, and they learn how to make healthy lifestyle choices—not just in the gym, or in the school, but in every aspect of their lives. Quite simply, what we are doing helps kids succeed. And what we do is something you can do!

It all starts with your vision. If you can take the first step of thinking hard about what you want to see in your program and outlining specific goals related to the desired outcomes, you have embarked on a PATH to success!

The PATH is more than the way to a high-quality physical education program. It's a strategy for positive and successful teaching.

■ **P** represents **planning**. No one can get to a destination without some kind of map; in the same way, you need to know where you want to go and figure out the best way to get there. Think of planning as mapping out your PATH to your goals.

■ **A** represents **activity**. Simply *moving* is a key to a healthy lifestyle! I will show you how you can reduce standing-around time in your gym and get students active in measurable ways.

■ **T** represents **technology**. We have so many devices available today that offer exciting opportunities for enhancing our curricula and improving our teaching. From GPS devices to mobile apps, I'll show you some of the countless ways you can use technology to get kids interested in their health and bring life to your gym.

■ **H** represents **harmony**. Two heads are better than one, and a whole team can accomplish so much more than one individual. I have been privileged to have many people involved in bringing a vision to life—colleagues, administrators, volunteers, parents, community members. You will see how reaching out to others can enhance your program and extend its success far beyond the gym walls!

Throughout this book, you'll get tips and strategies related to PATH that are based on my experience in building an award-winning program. Each chapter begins with "Approach the PATH," which describes how each of the four elements (planning, activity, technology, and harmony) applies to the chapter's topic. And each chapter closes with questions that challenge you to apply the four elements to the chapter's topic as you consider how you will implement related changes in your program. Throughout each chapter, "Ideas That Work" sidebars highlight tried-and-true tips for applying PATH to your own teaching. Finally, chapter 1 discusses how you can use PATH as a guide in building a program that makes a difference.

The rest of the book covers a sampling of topics that are common to physical education programs. Chapter 2 shows how you can design authentic assessments that give you meaningful information about your students' health. Armed with this information, you are equipped to set goals for their achievement and measure their progress.

Getting students moving in ways that interest them is key to bringing about lasting positive changes in their health. In chapter 3, I share three sample unit plans that demonstrate how lifestyle activities—in this case, snowshoeing, backpacking, and disc golf—can be integrated into your curriculum.

To make healthy lifestyle choices, students need to know what *healthy* means. I have incorporated fitness education into my daily curriculum by creating warm-ups that emphasize various fitness components (such as flexibility and muscular strength). Chapter 4 offers a sampling of these fitness warm-ups.

Heart rate monitors and pedometers have become a big part of my program, so much so that I've devoted an entire chapter (5) to describing how I use them! (If you don't currently have heart rate monitors and pedometers, and you fear you don't have funds to purchase them, don't worry—we even discuss ways you can get funding.)

At Hortonville, we're concerned about adults' health, not just kids'. I've extended some of the principles of teaching healthy lifestyles to staff wellness programs, and I share in chapter 6 how the programs work.

Finally, in chapter 7, I describe ways I've incorporated the teaching of healthy lifestyles that go beyond the gym. After-school programs and summer programming help you ensure that the lessons you're teaching will be implemented outside the school walls.

As physical educators, it is up to us to lead the way in making healthy lifestyles an important part of our school curriculum. A healthy future for our students should be our common goal. We have proved that healthy change is possible, and you can be part of the healthy lifestyle revolution!

Acknowledgments

I have been blessed to have so many supportive people in my life! First of all, Marshal, Michael, Jennie, and my mom, Sally. Second, I have had the privilege of teaching with two of the best physical educators in the country—Marcia Schmidt (Hortonville High School) and Cheryl Richardson (formerly of Hortonville Elementary School and now with NASPE). My school district has also been very supportive of teaching quality physical education, and my principal, John Brattlund, and associate principal, Janice Zuege, have always supported my vision! I have also been an active member in my state physical education association, WHPE, and its networking and learning opportunities have helped me along the PATH to success!

chapter 1

Getting Started

It's all about the PATH!

What is your vision for your physical education program? Close your eyes and imagine for a few minutes what you think teaching high-quality physical education would look like. What do you see? An exciting curriculum that your students respond to? A physical education class where everyone participates and everyone can succeed? A group of students who are getting healthier and more active?

Teaching high-quality physical education starts with your vision. Your vision for your program reflects what you are passionate about, and this passion motivates you to do all the hard work necessary for making positive changes. Defining your vision is necessary for outlining the goals that you want to accomplish; and then with realistic goals in mind, you can begin to make a plan to achieve them. One of the most important goals that you should be striving for is providing instruction that will help your students to lead healthy lifestyles. A healthy future for our students is one of the most important goals all physical educators should emphasize.

I had a vision for my middle school physical education program and was fortunate to work with two other teachers who shared that vision and fought for it every step of the way. Nothing worth achieving is easy. It takes hard work to mold a program into something you are proud of—and it is worth every minute you spend working on it. In this chapter you will read my part of an amazing story about how teachers can work together to achieve anything. Grab your vision and let's get started!

My Journey

Several years ago I began working with the two other physical educators in my district, Marcia Schmidt of Hortonville High School and Cheryl Richardson of Hortonville Elementary School, to identify improvements we could make in our program. We all thought that there was so much more we could be doing to provide physical education that helped our students live healthier lifestyles. The three of us embarked on a study of our program that resulted in several findings.

We discovered that our curriculum was not aligned with the state or national standards for physical education. It was clear to us that if we wanted to present a curriculum that represented high-quality physical education, it was imperative that we incorporate attention to these standards in our teaching. The national standards (NASPE 2004) show us specific ways of measuring what constitutes a physically educated student:

Standard 1: Demonstrates competency in motor skills and movement patterns needed to perform a variety of physical activities.

Standard 2: Demonstrates understanding of movement concepts, principles, strategies, and tactics as they apply to the learning and performance of physical activities.

Standard 3: Participates regularly in physical activity.

Standard 4: Achieves and maintains a health-enhancing level of physical fitness.

Standard 5: Exhibits responsible personal and social behavior that respects self and others in physical activity settings.

Standard 6: Values physical activity for health, enjoyment, challenge, self-expression, and/or social interaction.

So we decided that physical education standards would be our guide in writing a high-quality curriculum. We were also dissatisfied with the emphasis in our program on teaching team sports. In analyzing our curriculum, we found that we were teaching basketball and volleyball for 12 years! Now, there's certainly nothing wrong with teaching team sports, and in fact these sports should be part of a solid physical education program. But we were concerned that overemphasis on team sports tended to exclude the majority of students from the benefits that physical education has to offer, since it is mostly the more athletic students who enjoy and benefit from these units rather than the less-skilled students who might not be cut out for athletics but still can and should benefit from physical activity. Further, we believed we were missing an opportunity to expose students to activities they could and would do not only in PE class, but outside of class and well into their adult lives, such as golf, tennis, in-line skating, and backpacking.

Because our vision was to help students live healthy lifestyles, we agreed that it was important to provide information to our students about the components of a healthy lifestyle. We thought that our program's emphasis should be on providing our students with not only the skills but also the knowledge that they needed in order to lead a healthy lifestyle. Addressing the components of fitness in our curriculum became a goal, along with assessments that could give us meaningful information about what students were learning.

Finally, we resolved to increase the use of technology and good old-fashioned activity in our program. We set a goal for students to be engaged in moderate to vigorous activity at least 50 percent of our class time. Further, we believed that the use of heart rate monitors and pedometers offered exciting possibilities for both incorporating technology and increasing activity. These tools also presented another means of authentic assessment that would tell us whether our students were truly getting healthier.

In 2001, we found out about a grant called the Carol M. White Physical Education Program (PEP) grant. As described in the preface, this program makes grants available to schools and organizations that seek to improve the health of K-12 students. We realized that this was a fantastic opportunity to get much-needed financial help to make the big changes we dreamed of.

The first step in writing a proposal was to agree on our vision and goal. Since we had gone through the self-evaluation process, we knew what the weaknesses were and how we wanted to fix them. That process was driven by our desire to bring high-quality physical education to our school district. Teaching high-quality physical education has many components. It includes the national physical education standards, lifetime activities, knowledge of the components required for leading a healthy lifestyle, authentic assessment, technology that can be used in authentically assessing students (such

Cheryl Richardson (left) and Marcia Schmidt (right) worked tirelessly with me to see our vision become reality!

as pedometers and heart rate monitors), and lessons that engage students in moderate to vigorous activity for at least 50 percent of class time.

In writing our proposal, we outlined the specific problems we wanted to address in our program, then suggested the solutions we wanted to implement with the help of the grant:

- Implement a curriculum that incorporated the national and state physical education standards.
- Improve assessment techniques.
- Increase community involvement and interest in our program.

We spent six weeks together writing the grant with help from Tricia Sarvella, my friend and neighbor. In the fall of 2001 we received word that we had won the PEP grant! Here is the announcement of the grant, which describes what we were seeking to do:

> After a critical evaluation conducted by the physical education program in the Hortonville School District, several profound weaknesses were identified in their physical education curriculum. One particular weakness is that their current instruction is not aligned with the national and state physical education standards. Other identified areas of weakness include the lack of knowledge of fitness concepts and overall physical fitness, substandard methods of assessment, and inadequate community involvement in the physical education department. *Fitness Education: The Shape of Things to Come,* the project proposed by the Hortonville physical education department, is fundamentally different from the stereotypical "roll out the ball and play" classes of decades past that featured little meaningful instruction. *The goal of the project is to improve the overall physical fitness and development of the students in the Hortonville School District by (a) implementing a curriculum that incorporates state and national standards; (b) improving assessment techniques; and (c) increasing community interest and involvement in their physical education program.*

Winning the PEP grant has changed our program in so many important ways. It provided time for our K-12 physical education teaching staff to rewrite our entire physical education curriculum. Our curriculum now has a K-12 scope and sequence, addresses the national physical education teaching standards, teaches the five components of fitness, includes technology (pedometers and heart rate monitors), and emphasizes lifetime activities and teaching of healthy lifestyles. The inclusion of lifetime activities such as snowshoeing and disc golf not only has provided class time for our students to participate in these activities but also has resulted in something unexpected and very positive: Several students have gone home after an enjoyable day of snowshoeing and asked their parents to purchase snowshoes for their families—and their parents did purchase the equipment!

The grant has provided funding for purchasing the needed equipment so that our students do not have to wait in line to use it. The result of having enough equipment for each of our students to use is an emphasis on being moderately to vigorously active for at least 50 percent of class time. The grant also has provided us funds for purchasing a variety of lifetime activity equipment that can be used at various grade levels. Because of the grant funding, our emphasis now is on lifetime activity and not only team sports as in the past. Our students also are using heart rate monitors and pedometers. The heart rate monitors provide the students with instant feedback on exercising in a target heart rate zone, and the pedometers inform students whether they are achieving their step goals. The results of using this technology are also the awareness of the importance of being lifetime movers and not couch potatoes! The students in our classes know the importance of taking at least 10,000 steps a day, and they know they should be exercising at least 60 minutes every day. Our teaching staff is also using the technology to authentically assess students on their fitness levels—not grading them on whether they are wearing the correct T-shirt and shorts to class!

The grant not only has influenced the physical education teaching staff in our school district but also has provided a model for other school districts in our state. The fact that Cheryl, Marcia, and I wrote the PEP grant by ourselves provided the inspiration to other programs in our state (that is, if we could do it, anyone else could). This is not a put-down to the three of us but a statement that if you have a vision and work hard, you can achieve anything.

Your PATH

You don't have to win a grant to make positive changes in your program. It's true that resources are always needed, but changes don't start with resources; they start with vision, and they continue with hard work. And vision and hard work are free! It's so important not to get discouraged by the potential obstacles. Instead, start with a vision you can believe in, and make a realistic plan for bringing about the changes you want to see. And starting small is OK!

At the beginning of this chapter I asked you to close your eyes and envision the type of physical education program you want to teach. Has your vision changed now that you have read about the PEP grant and my school? If yes, what does your vision look like now? Write down your vision for including concepts of a healthy lifestyle in your classes. And then write down one or two goals you can accomplish right now to teach healthy lifestyles in your classes. Is there a lesson that you already teach and that you can adapt so that it includes a concept of healthy lifestyles? Writing down your goals and looking at one of your current lessons can provide you with a model to use in including concepts of healthy lifestyles in other lessons that you teach.

In addition to focusing on the importance of vision, following the PATH will help you improve the health of your students. As explained in the preface, PATH stands for four strategies that have helped me to emphasize healthy lifestyles in my physical education program: planning, activity, technology, and harmony. Throughout this book, PATH serves as a way of thinking about and highlighting teaching approaches that are proven to work.

Planning

I have found that it is vital to give time and attention to planning ways to achieve my program goals. Change doesn't just happen, and good teaching doesn't just happen! You must constantly assess the learning that is taking place in your students so you can know whether what you are doing is working. When you know what your students are learning (and what they are not learning), you can adjust your curriculum or other aspects of your teaching to see if you get better results. Throughout this book, you'll discover ways that planning can help you.

Activity

For some students, their physical education class is the only time of the day they get any meaningful activity. I have found that maximizing the time that students spend moving in my gym is one way to improve their health. Not only do they accumulate steps and work their bodies, but they also become part of a culture where activity and movement are valued and practiced. This gives them the skill and confidence to carry the lessons they are learning in physical education outside the gym walls. I'll show you tips for keeping kids moving as much as possible while in your physical education class.

Technology

There is no denying the appeal of gadgets and devices to students. Mobile phones, personal computers, televisions—it's hard to keep a kid away from a screen. Normally we think of these devices as the enemy of an active life—but there's no reason why we can't turn them into an asset that promotes activity and makes pursuing a healthy lifestyle easier and more fun. The possibilities are endless: Use GPS units to make a heart-healthy hike more fun. Offer pedometers to help students set goals and monitor their progress. Create a physical education website full of information and resources for your students and their families. As you read this book, you'll see many more ways to creatively incorporate the use of technology in your classes to get kids engaged and help you assess learning.

Harmony

Harmony describes a teaching approach that emphasizes cooperation with teachers and other adults, integrated learning, and the extension of learning beyond the school environment. The emphasis on healthy lifestyles in my school district has definitely been a team effort—not only among the physical education teachers but also among the classroom teachers, administration, parents, and community. It was really important for us to include our community when writing the PEP grant. Not only did we want our students to learn the importance of living a healthy lifestyle, but we also wanted our students to bring that information into the community. So throughout this book, when I talk about harmony, I'm talking about the ways you can extend your curriculum beyond your classroom. For example, you could work with a science teacher in offering collaborative lessons on how the cardiorespiratory system works or in identifying types of leaves on a nature hike. You could ask parents about the activities their families enjoy, and plan a unit on one or more of the activities mentioned. Or you could offer activities for your students to do after school or throughout the summer. The possibilities are endless!

Summary

You can have a vision of what high-quality physical education should look like and develop your program so that you achieve those goals. We tell our students, "If you dream it, you can achieve it!" As physical educators, we need to take those words and apply them to our vision of teaching healthy lifestyles. You don't have to win a grant to achieve the goal of including healthy lifestyle education in your physical education program. What you *do* need is a vision to inspire your students to lead a healthy lifestyle. With your vision in mind, you can start on the PATH to teaching your students the importance of leading a healthy lifestyle. Now let's get started!

Reference

National Association for Sport and Physical Education. (2004). *Moving into the future: National standards for physical education.* 2nd ed. Reston, VA: Author.

Beyond Dressing Out

Use authentic assessment to find out how healthy your students are (or aren't)!

Would you like to grade your students in ways that go beyond dressing out? Are you tired of getting out your red pen and subtracting points as soon as your students set foot in the gym without the correct uniform? If you read the physical education standards provided by the National Association for Sport and Physical Education (NASPE), you'll find no mention of what students wear! So how did these practices get started, and why do we care so much about them? Isn't the goal of physical education to help our students enjoy moving, learn as much as they can about healthy living, and explore various sports and fitness activities in order to find a form of movement that they enjoy? If so, then certainly these goals should be reflected in the assessments we use. With this in mind, *authentic assessment*—assessment that doesn't just produce a grade but also provides useful feedback about what your students are learning—is a crucial part of building a program that truly helps your students become healthier.

In this chapter, I show you how I have assessed students in a way that tells me that they are (or are not) getting healthier. Whether you are a new teacher or a seasoned physical educator, you will find something in this chapter to help you to go beyond dressing out!

Approach the PATH . . .

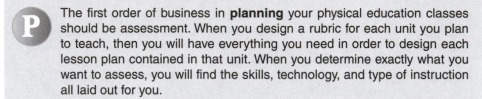

P The first order of business in **planning** your physical education classes should be assessment. When you design a rubric for each unit you plan to teach, then you will have everything you need in order to design each lesson plan contained in that unit. When you determine exactly what you want to assess, you will find the skills, technology, and type of instruction all laid out for you.

A The goal of each lesson you teach should be to have your students engage in moderate or vigorous **activity** for at least 50 percent of class time. You can assess your students' level of engagement in many ways. For example, you can start a stopwatch when activity begins and pause it each time your class stops to listen to instructions from you; at the end of the class period, the accumulated time shown on your stopwatch should meet the goal of devoting at least 50 percent of class time to moderate or vigorous activity. If it doesn't, then you are using too much class time in giving instructions. You can also assess movement through the use of pedometers. At the start of each class, set a goal for the total number of steps that every student should take, then check each student's pedometer to see if he or she met the goal. These are just a couple of examples of how activity can be assessed.

T Beyond stopwatches and pedometers, you can use **technology** in many other ways to assess each student's progress. For example, you can use digital cameras and digital video cameras to establish a visual record of each student performing the skills you want to assess. You can also use heart rate monitors to assess a student's heart rate during any activity. You can combine information gained through pedometers and heart rate monitors to see if your students are being moderately to vigorously active for at least 50 percent of class time.

H If you want your entire school district's physical education teaching staff to work in **harmony**, it is crucial that you use common assessments (such as rubrics). A good assessment tool also includes information about how each NASPE standard is being assessed; this information can be used to show administrators and parents what high-quality physical education looks like and how it is being assessed!

I structure my assessments on the basis of four categories: heart rate monitor data, lifetime fitness goal setting, written activity, and physical activity. Table 2.1 shows how each category figures into a student's grade, as well as the NASPE standards addressed by the category. I find that this structure works well; it not only gives me the information I need in order to assess how my students are doing but also provides feedback to my students.

TABLE 2.1

Sample Assessment Structure

Assessment category	Percentage of grade	NASPE standard(s) addressed
Lifetime fitness goal setting results	10	3, 4
Written activity	10	2
Heart rate monitor data	30	3, 4
Physical activity	50 (25 each for two units of instruction)	1, 2, 5, 6

Heart Rate Monitors

Heart rate monitors offer you a wonderful tool for authentic assessment. When students wear them during activity, the monitors provide objective information that not only tells you what students are achieving but also helps the students learn what their bodies should feel like when working out by allowing them to equate the heart rate shown on their monitor to the level of exertion when they exercise. Students can then apply this understanding when doing activity—anytime and anywhere—and eventually become able to exercise in their target heart rate zone without the monitor's help!

Note: Some students may take medications that affect their heart rate. Because of the private nature of health information, you will need to contact the student's parents with any questions you have in this regard.

At the beginning of the school year, I give all of my classes specific

Using a heart rate monitor during physical activity helps students understand what their bodies should feel like when they are being active in their target heart rate zone.

instruction on cardiorespiratory fitness, resting heart rate, and target heart rate zone. These concepts are so important that part of my students' heart rate monitor grade is determined by a rubric assessing their command of this information (see figure 2.1). The other part of the grade depends on results of a 20-minute workout performed while wearing a heart rate monitor; the goal here is for the student to keep his or her heart rate in the target zone for the entire 20 minutes. The rubric, workout, and scoring system are discussed further a bit later in this chapter.

After teaching the concepts, I use heart rate monitors to gather each student's resting heart rate data, which can be used to calculate his or her target heart rate zone. To get a resting heart rate, the student lies on his or her back while wearing the heart rate monitor on one arm, which is extended and resting on the floor. (Any students who cannot get a heart rate while lying down can do this activity while sitting up with the arm wearing the monitor resting at their side.) The student's partner sits beside him or her while holding a sheet of paper labeled with the student's name and featuring vertical numbering from one to six listed down the left side of the paper. These numbers represent 1-minute increments. When all students and their partners have assumed the correct positions, you start a stopwatch and then prompt the recording partners to note their student's heart rate at each 1-minute interval during a 6-minute period. These 6 heart rate readings will be averaged to calculate their resting heart rate. The students then switch roles and repeat the process so that everyone has recorded a resting heart rate.

Once the students know their resting heart rate, they can use it to calculate their target heart rate zone as follows:

Ideas That Work!

H Integrate heart rate monitors and math! I talk to all the math teachers at my school and ask if they would be willing to integrate calculation of target heart rate into their classes. This approach has been successful, and I have found that it works best if I minimize any work that the math teacher has to do. Here's how I do that: I get a class list from each math teacher, then put all of my students into categories according to the math class they are in. This way, the math teacher has all of the students' papers ready for the lesson. I also provide the math teachers with the formula for calculating target heart rate zone, make sure that they are comfortable with doing the project, and answer any questions they have.

1. Find your maximum heart rate by subtracting your age from 220; for example, $220 - 12 = 208$.

2. Subtract your resting heart rate from your maximum heart rate; for example, $208 - 72 = 136$.

3. To find the lower limit of your target heart rate zone, multiply the number you got in step 2 by 0.6 (to represent 60 percent), then add your resting heart rate: for example, $136 \times 0.6 = 82 + 72 = 154$.

4. To find the upper limit of your target heart rate zone, multiply the number you got in step 2 by 0.9 (to represent 90 percent), then add your resting heart rate; for example, $136 \times 0.9 = 122 + 72 = 194$.

Thus a student with these numbers should aim to exercise at an intensity that keeps his or her heart rate between 154 and 194 beats per minute.

Once you know each student's target heart rate zone, you can have them work out in their zone for 20 minutes while wearing a heart rate monitor. Choose any aerobic activity for this workout—the sky is the limit! Play soccer, run laps around a track, jump rope, hula hoop, or ride an exercise bike, to name a few. This workout and the rubric that assesses students' knowledge of heart rate concepts (see figure 2.1) form the basis for the students' heart rate monitor grade. The rubric is worth up to 12 points, and time spent working out in the target heart rate zone is worth up to 20 points (1 point per minute) for a total of 32 points. For example, in one 20-minute workout, if a student scores 9 points on the rubric and spends 18 minutes in his or her target heart zone as recorded by the heart rate monitor, the student's score would be 27 points.

Our heart rate monitor workouts are done during a special activity that I call Fitness Friday. (My students also have practice times for using heart rate monitors at the beginning of the school year; during these practices, they are not graded, and they start out with 5- to 10-minute workouts.) Each Friday, when the students come to physical education class, they come out of the locker room and immediately put on their heart rate monitor and pedometer. I give the class brief instructions about the length of their heart rate monitor workout and review the fitness activities that they will do after their workout. (These fitness activities are discussed further in chapter 4.)

FIGURE 2.1

Rubric for 20-Minute Heart Rate Monitor

Name _____

Student knowledge	6 points	3 points	0 points	
Heart rate and heart rate monitor	Student correctly describes (orally or in writing) *both* proper placement of the heart rate monitor on the body *and* how information about heart rate can be used outside of PE class.	Student describes (orally or in writing) *either* proper placement of the heart rate monitor on the body *or* how information about heart rate can be used outside of PE class.	Student correctly describes *neither* proper placement of the heart rate monitor on the body *nor* how information about heart rate can be used outside of PE class.	
Target heart rate zone	Student correctly describes (orally or in writing) *both* the target rate heart zone used in class *and* strategies for maintaining target heart rate while exercising.	Student correctly describes (orally or in writing) *either* the target heart rate zone used in class *or* strategies for maintaining target heart rate while exercising.	Student correctly describes *neither* the target heart rate zone used in class *nor* strategies for maintaining target heart rate while exercising.	
			TOTAL	

From C. Gorwitz, 2012, *Teaching healthy lifestyles in middle school PE: Strategies from an award-winning program* (Champaign, IL: Human Kinetics).

Using heart rate monitors as a form of grading gives me important information about the cardiorespiratory fitness of my students. I use this information to design lessons that incorporate the correct level of cardiorespiratory endurance for each of my classes. The monitors also provide concrete information that I can share with parents about their student's cardiorespiratory fitness. When parents ask questions about how their student's grade is calculated, I share the heart rate monitor score and explain that the student's grade is based on how long he or she worked out in the target heart rate zone.

Heart rate monitors also give students immediate benefits. In addition to helping them learn what their target heart rate zone feels like, the feedback from the monitor can be a source of encouragement as students see the improvement in their own fitness. It also provides a positive experience in physical education for all students, no matter their body size or fitness level, because each student is working out in his or her target zone. Thus, for example, overweight students can enjoy a positive exercise experience and receive a high grade by exercising in their own target zone.

Using the monitors can even alert you to potential health problems in your students. For example, as soon as one particular student put on the heart rate monitor, the student's heart rate skyrocketed. I contacted the student's parents, who consulted a doctor and found out that the student had a previously unidentified cardiac problem.

Lifetime Fitness Goal Setting

I use physical fitness testing as a means for teaching students how to set goals for improving their health. An example of an assessment for goal setting is shown in figure 2.2. This assessment is flexible enough that it can accommodate many different types of tests in the various areas of fitness (cardiorespiratory endurance, muscular strength, muscular endurance, flexibility, and body composition and nutrition) since teachers use a wide variety of fitness tests. However, you may want to use this as a template or guide for creating a more specific assessment of your own. It's very important that goals be specific and measurable, and customizing a form allows you to make it more meaningful for the tests you use.

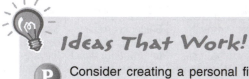

Ideas That Work!

P Consider creating a personal fitness goal sheet for your students. They can set goals for improvement in flexibility, strength, and nutrition—whatever you think they need! When students define and write goals for their own fitness improvement, they are more likely to pursue and attain them.

FIGURE 2.2

Sample Lifetime Fitness Goal Assessment

At the beginning of each quarter I discuss the importance of setting goals and their importance in leading a healthy lifestyle. I emphasize that each area of fitness (cardiorespiratory endurance, muscular strength, muscular endurance, flexibility, and body composition and nutrition) is of equal importance in achieving a healthy lifestyle. Each student fills out the Lifetime Fitness Goal Assessment and performs the fitness test that goes along with that area of fitness. I have provided a generic goal sheet so that teachers can use the fitness test of their choosing for each area. (For example, I use the Fitnessgram PACER test to assess cardiorespiratory fitness, but other teachers might use different tests to assess this area.)

Name _____

Circle the quarter   1   2   3   4

CARDIORESPIRATORY GOALS

My goal for this quarter for the PACER:

Laps _____

Zone _____

PACER TEST RESULTS

Laps finished _____

Zone _____

Perceived exertion (circle one)   1   2   3   4   5   6   7   8   9   10

I will do the following exercises outside my physical education class to improve my cardio-respiratory fitness this quarter:

_____

_____ Number of times each week _____

_____

_____ Number of times each week _____

_____

_____ Number of times each week _____

STRENGTH GOALS

My strength goal for this quarter is to do the following: _____

_____

_____

_____

I will do the following exercises outside my physical education class to improve my strength this quarter:

_____

_____ Number of times each week _____

(continued)

From C. Gorwitz, 2012, *Teaching healthy lifestyles in middle school PE: Strategies from an award-winning program* (Champaign, IL: Human Kinetics).

_____

_____ Number of times each week _____

_____

_____ Number of times each week _____

My end-of-the-quarter strength test results were: _____

Perceived exertion (circle one)   1   2   3   4   5   6   7   8   9   10

FLEXIBILITY GOALS

My flexibility goal for this quarter is to do the following: _____

_____

_____

_____.

I will do the following exercises outside my physical education class to improve my flexibility this quarter:

_____

_____ Number of times each week _____

_____

_____ Number of times each week _____

_____

_____ Number of times each week _____

My end-of-the-quarter flexibility test results are _____

Perceived exertion (circle one)   1   2   3   4   5   6   7   8   9   10

NUTRITION GOALS

My goal for healthy eating this quarter is: _____

_____

_____

_____

At the end of the quarter, I will assess my progress:

Did I reach my goal for healthy eating? (circle one) Yes   No

If I didn't achieve my goal, what stopped me from achieving this goal? _____

_____

_____

_____

_____.

From C. Gorwitz, 2012, *Teaching healthy lifestyles in middle school PE: Strategies from an award-winning program* (Champaign, IL: Human Kinetics).

Writing Activity

A written assignment can involve anything you want it to, as long as it gives you a realistic picture of your students' knowledge of the concepts you are teaching. It also offers a great way to incorporate communication skills in your physical education curriculum! I believe that writing activities help my students know that they do not have to be the most skilled athlete in order to succeed in my classes. My students know that there is more than one way to show me that they understand key concepts. They do not have to make 10 free throws in order to get an A in physical education, and if they can describe how to shoot a free throw, they will be more likely to try, because the assessment is meaningful to them. I want them to have the interest and self-confidence to go out in their driveways and shoot baskets and know that this is a good way to get their sixty minutes of daily exercise. The other concept I want them to understand is that they don't have to be on a formal basketball team or be the most skilled basketball player to enjoy getting outside and shooting baskets in their driveway. Giving students a chance to write about key concepts helps them develop the confidence to try new things.

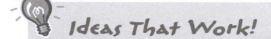

Ideas That Work!

P Encourage improvement with portfolios! I keep a portfolio for each of my students, and I keep the collection of portfolios in a wheeled crate so that I can easily roll it out into the gym when they are needed in class. Each student's portfolio includes his or her PACER score sheets and personal fitness goal sheets. Reviewing their portfolios helps students see their progress and encourages them to continue improving.

For each unit I teach, students turn in written work at least three times. The written assessments address the main areas in which I want to evaluate my students: knowledge of strategy and key concepts, fitness, and sporting behavior. Figure 2.3 on page 18 shows a written assessment used for a pickleball unit. It covers strategy first by asking students to provide a written description of key concepts in pickleball. This work has really helped my students think about different strategies they can use during the activity—and helped them choose strategies while playing, rather than waiting for me to tell them what to do. It has also helped me evaluate how well my students can apply key concepts in a game situation. Next, the assessment checks fitness and activity level by asking students to report how hard they feel they worked during the activity (i.e., to report their perceived exertion) and how many pedometer steps they took. Perceived exertion not only tends to provide an accurate measure of effort but also prompts the student to consider and assess the activity and his or her effort in doing it. Finally, the assessment addresses sporting behavior. Focusing on this element has made a real difference in my students' conduct; for example, many teams start their games by shaking hands or clapping their pickleball rackets at the net before play begins!

FIGURE 2.3

Pickleball Assessment

Name_____ Partner _____

STRATEGY (10 POINTS)

Name two strategies that you used during this pickleball match (5 points each):

1.

2.

Standard 2: Demonstrates understanding of movement concepts, principles, strategies, and tactics as they apply to the learning and performance of physical activities.

FITNESS (5 POINTS EACH)

How hard did you work during the game? Circle the number that best describes the exercise you got from this game.

1 = I didn't work hard at all

2 = I worked some, but walked for most of the game

3 = I worked hard and only had to walk a couple of times

4 = I worked hard and only had to walk once

5 = I worked to the best of my ability and never stopped to walk or take a time out

1 2 3 4 5

How many pedometer steps did you take? _____

Standard 4: Achieves and maintains a health-enhancing level of physical fitness.

SPORTING BEHAVIOR (5 POINTS)

Describe an example of good sporting behavior that you saw another student doing or that you did during your match.

Standard 5: Exhibits responsible personal and social behavior that respects self and others in physical activity settings.

From C. Gorwitz, 2012, *Teaching healthy lifestyles in middle school PE: Strategies from an award-winning program* (Champaign, IL: Human Kinetics).

Physical Activity

During each 9-week quarter, I teach two activities (sports or games) that are graded. I teach other activities as well, but the chosen two are graded formally. The rubric for each of these two activities is worth 25 percent of a student's grade (thus 50 percent together).

Figure 2.4 on page 20 shows a rubric that I use for sixth-grade football. I chose football for the example because most teachers include it in their curriculum; thus, it is likely to give you a good sense of how you can use this type of rubric in your own classes. I use the same rubric format for all activities that I teach except dance which assesses different areas (e.g., sporting behavior is not assessed during the dance unit). I use these rubrics to assess my students in three different areas: strategy and key concepts, fitness, and sporting behavior. Each section of the rubric also includes the NASPE standard being assessed in that section. Before beginning instruction, I give each student a blank rubric so that they know how they will be assessed.

Skill

Skill is worth 3 points in the rubric, which lists the skills to be assessed and the relevant NASPE standards (i.e., standards 1 and 2). The students are taught each skill and given plenty of time to practice it before being assessed on it. I do assessment during the game portion of the sport or activity by walking around and assessing each student on each day of game play, then giving them a score based on the rubric. The grades are then averaged to produce the final skill grade.

Strategy and Good Sporting Behavior

Strategy and good sporting behavior are worth a total of 6 points in the rubric. In this category, students choose before the unit starts which point value they are going to achieve. Very few students choose to go for fewer than 6 points, but I allow them to choose because it gives students an example of the types of choices and consequences they will face as adults. If they choose a low point value they will get a low grade, and this type of thing can be expected in other areas of life as well—if they do not put forth effort, they will not realize benefits. If students never have a time that they practice making good, healthy choices they will never do that in real life. I allow them to choose to draw, explain orally, or write about their

Ideas That Work!

H I engage my students in the assessment process by providing them with several choices as to how they can demonstrate mastery of the content covered in class. They can choose to write, provide information orally, or draw. Having a choice helps students feel more confident and encourages them to put forth strong effort in learning key concepts. There are many different learning styles out there, and giving students some say in how they present information to you empowers them to become successful, healthy learners!

FIGURE 2.4

Sixth-Grade Football Rubric

Name _____

Area assessed	Advanced	Proficient	Basic	
Skill—NASPE standards 1 and 2	3 points	2 points	1 point	
Throw	Grips the ball with thumb and index finger on back and other fingers on laces, and nondominant side faces target. Steps forward with the foot opposite the throwing arm.	Grips the ball with thumb and index finger in the middle of the ball, and nondominant side faces target 80 percent of the time. Steps forward with the foot opposite the throwing arm.	Grips the ball with thumb and index finger not on the back of the ball, and nondominant side does not face target. Steps forward with same-side foot as throwing arm.	
Spiral	Ball spirals tightly through the air on release.	Ball does not spiral tightly.	Ball wobbles through the air.	
Follow-through	Arm goes across body with pinky coming off last.	Arm does not go across body with pinky coming off last.	Arm goes directly down the side of the body.	
Catch	Catches the ball 90 percent of the time or better with hands out away from the body.	Catches the ball 80 percent of the time with hands halfway out from the body.	Catches the ball less than 50 percent of the time; hands are not out away from the body.	
			TOTAL	
Strategy and good sporting behavior—NASPE standards 2 and 5	6 points	3 points	1 point	
Written work	Describes three strategies used during a football game.	Describes two strategies used during a football game.	Describes one strategy used during a football game.	
	Describes three types of good sporting behavior that the student will use during game play.	Describes two types of good sporting behavior that the student will use during game play.	Describes one type of good sporting behavior that the student will use during game play.	
			TOTAL	
Fitness—NASPE standards 3, 4, and 6	6 points	3 points	1 point	
Pedometer step count (average the pedometer scores recorded three times during the unit)	3,000 or more	2,999–2,500	2,499 or fewer	
Written work	Describes how three or more components of fitness can be achieved during game play.	Describes how two components of fitness can be achieved during game play.	Describes how one component of fitness can be achieved during game play.	
			TOTAL	
			TOTAL SCORE	

From C. Gorwitz, 2012, *Teaching healthy lifestyles in middle school PE: Strategies from an award-winning program* (Champaign, IL: Human Kinetics).

strategies and how they are going to show good sporting behavior during each activity. Each category also lists the national standard to be assessed (i.e., NASPE standards 2 and 5). I have a basket filled with strategy papers that students can take and work on outside of class or during the first few minutes of class before everyone is out of the locker room and ready to start. These strategy papers contain questions that are specific to the unit being taught (e.g., the strategy paper for pickleball asks students about what strategy they would use to successfully return the ball to their opponent). I also set equipment and written worksheets out for students to use during the first few minutes of each class.

Figure 2.5 shows a goal sheet for strategy and good sporting behavior that a student can fill out for that portion of the rubric. Merely selecting a certain point value does not guarantee that the student will earn that full value. The student must describe the level of strategy and sporting behavior that he or she wants to achieve—and then actually achieve it!

FIGURE 2.5

Strategy and Sporting Behavior Goals: Football

Name _____

Circle your choice of how to present the information: writing, oral presentation, drawing.

1. Describe or draw two or three strategies you can use to get open so that the quarterback can throw you the ball.

2. Describe or draw two or three ways in which your team will use good sporting behavior during each football game.

If you are describing the strategy by means of oral presentation, take this paper to your teacher and describe the strategy to him or her. The teacher will then decide on the point values.

From C. Gorwitz, 2012, *Teaching healthy lifestyles in middle school PE: Strategies from an award-winning program* (Champaign, IL: Human Kinetics).

Fitness

This portion of the assessment addresses NASPE standards 3, 4, and 6. Students in my classes wear a pedometer every day, and daily step count goals are posted in the gym. I also discuss with the students why the step count is set the way it is for each lesson. For example, playing volleyball would not involve a very high step count, because it is not a cardiorespiratory activity. I lead a discussion with students about the cardiorespiratory endurance level required in a particular activity and the resulting step count specified for that lesson. In a way, discussion of the step count for the lesson is just as important as the number of steps the students end up taking. They need to know, for example, that if an activity is not going to involve a high level of cardiorespiratory endurance, the warm-up portion of the class will include an activity that requires a higher level of cardiorespiratory endurance.

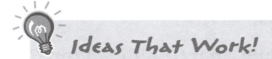

Ideas That Work!

P Set realistic step count goals for your students! When you start to use step count goals for assessment, you will first need to have your students wear a pedometer for several class periods so that you can gather step counts and decide what levels to use in your rubrics. Remember that you want *all* of your students to be successful, which means that you should set your step count goals at a realistic level!

Students also need to know the five components of fitness—cardiorespiratory endurance, muscular strength, muscular endurance, flexibility, and body composition and nutrition—and why they are important. Each lesson I teach begins by addressing one of these five components as a warm-up activity. (See chapter 4 for descriptions of some of these fitness warm-ups.) For a given activity, students choose which levels of step count they want to achieve, as well as the number of fitness components they will describe. Figure 2.6 shows a fitness goal sheet that a student can fill out for the fitness portion of the rubric.

FIGURE 2.6 ▭▭▭▭▭▭▭▭▭▭▭▭▭▭▭▭▭▭▭▭▭▭▭▭▭▭

Fitness Goals: Football

Name _____

1. Select the point value for the number of steps you are going to take today.

6 points (3,000 steps or more)   3 points (2,999–2,500 steps)   1 point (2,499 steps or fewer)

2. Circle the number of fitness components you are going to describe for this activity.

3 components   2 components   1 component

3. Circle the form in which you are going to share your description of the component(s) of fitness.

Oral   Drawing a picture   Written

4. Describe or draw the fitness component(s).

If you are orally describing the strategy, take this paper to your teacher and describe the strategy to him or her. The teacher will then decide on the point values.

From C. Gorwitz, 2012, *Teaching healthy lifestyles in middle school PE: Strategies from an award-winning program* (Champaign, IL: Human Kinetics).

Summary

Authentic assessments can encourage students to be active for a lifetime. You can incorporate authentic assessment into your program by designing rubrics that address the NASPE physical education standards, activity (pedometer steps), and knowledge. Using the authentic assessment tools in this chapter will give your students important feedback about leading a healthy lifestyle, and help instill the confidence to start making the choice to be healthy for a lifetime.

Challenge Questions

P How can you start using authentic assessments in your physical education classes? Think about the units you teach and start with one unit in which to develop an authentic assessment tool. Which unit are you going to start with? How can you plan the units that you teach to emphasize a healthy lifestyle?

A How are you going to assess the activities you teach to help students gain the self-confidence to lead a healthy lifestyle? How can you modify the current activities that you teach so that you can include authentic assessment tools?

T How can you use technology to assess student performance? Do you have pedometers that you can use? Are you ready to start using daily step count goals in your classes to assess moderate to vigorous activity levels? How can you include heart rate monitors into your classes?

H Does everyone on your physical education teaching staff use common assessments? If not, what plan of action can you use to get all of your teachers on board? What types of authentic assessment can you start to include in your physical education program? Write down the names of people at your school that you can use as a resource to learn more about authentic assessment.

chapter 3

Unit Plans for a Lifetime

Moving beyond sport leads to motivated lifetime movers!

One of the main goals of teaching physical education is to motivate our students to become lifetime movers. The heart of this effort lies in the units we plan! We should all take a look at our units through our students' eyes. Do the activities we teach and the games we play truly motivate and interest our students? Are we teaching what we're comfortable with instead of what our students enjoy? Are we too focused on sports that only a small percentage of our students will choose to use for movement activity in their free time?

As physical educators, we know better than anyone how many ways there are to move and be active. We have an amazing opportunity to share this knowledge and experience with students who might otherwise think that an active and healthy lifestyle is only for athletes! What better way to take advantage of this opportunity than to plan units featuring unique lifetime activities that our students *want* to do?

You can start including lifetime activities by asking a simple question: What do my students like to do outside of school? Thinking about this question will help you discover activities that you could start using in your classes to excite and motivate your students to become lifetime movers. Start out by adding one lifetime activity to your curriculum to pique your students' interest. Soon, they will want more!

Approach the PATH . . .

 What lifetime activities are most popular in your community? When **planning** which lifetime activities to include in your physical education curriculum, think about how to motivate students in your classes to use the lifetime activity skills you teach when they are outside of class. What better way is there to motivate our students to become lifetime movers than to include lifetime activities in the physical education curriculum? To find out what lifetime activities interest your students and their parents, consider putting together a simple survey to allow both students and parents to tell you what they would like to learn more about.

 Most students are not going to play team sports such as basketball or football in their leisure time when they are older. More likely, they will choose to participate in lifetime **activities** such as hiking, backpacking, golf, and disc golf. This is why it is so important to give your students opportunities to learn lifetime skills at an early age. Students are more willing to try something new when they are younger and excited about participating in activities outside of school! Examples of how to teach lifetime activities are provided in this chapter.

 You can include **technology** in many ways when teaching lifetime activities. For example, many software applications for electronic devices now include video clips showing how to perform lifetime activities. Students can also use heart rate monitors and pedometers for a lifetime. You don't have to be an expert in technology to include it in your lifetime activity lesson plans. Your students can even help you find types of technology that can be used to achieve the goal of becoming lifetime movers!

 One important step in the planning process is to work in **harmony** with others in your community. For example, if you are teaching golf, you might seek a local golf pro who is willing to come to your class to teach one lesson. Many people in your community would be willing to volunteer if you just ask!

In this chapter, I show you how I incorporated into my program three lifetime activities that my students tend to do with their families in Wisconsin: snowshoeing, disc golf, and backpacking. You will learn what has worked in my classes and how to apply this approach to any other lifetime activities that you would like to teach.

Snowshoeing

My snowshoeing unit has been a big hit in my Wisconsin school, where we have long winters and lots of snow! It works as a lifetime activity in my school for two reasons. First, it's something that students and their families can choose to do outside of PE class. Several students have asked for snowshoes as a present from their parents so that they can go out and do what we have done in class on their own time. Some parents have purchased snowshoes for their entire family after their son or daughter has come home from an exhilarating day of snowshoeing in PE class! (But you don't have to live in a cold climate to teach this unit—I have talked with teachers who have taught snowshoeing on grass!)

The second reason that snowshoeing works as a lifetime activity is that it provides plenty of opportunity for heart-healthy movement that is *fun*. Students wear pedometers during the snowshoeing activities and games so that they can set and achieve fitness goals; for example, they might aim to take 3,000 steps in one class day's activity. (This also makes for easy assessment!) While they're doing fun things like hiking and relay races in their snowshoes, they're burning calories and building healthy bodies!

Unit Overview

I teach a 3-day unit on snowshoeing. What follows here is a basic description of how I organize the unit, but this is only one of many possible ways.

My students love snowshoeing!

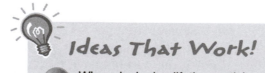

Ideas That Work!

P When designing lifetime activity units, select a theme for each day of the lesson to help you organize the important skills and activities that you want to teach each day. Before you start planning your units, come up with ideas for themes that will pique your students' interest even as they highlight the skills and activities you want to teach.

- Day 1. The theme I use for the first day is Enjoying the Great Outdoors. To introduce the unit, I start with the most important things: safety and fitness! First, we discuss the importance of layering clothing for outdoor winter activity, as well as how to put on and take off snowshoes quickly and securely. The next step is to talk about the calorie-burning benefits of snowshoeing and set step count goals for the day's activity. Then, after strapping on our pedometers, it's time for simple introductory activities: a scavenger hunt in the snow, a nature hike, or even making snowpeople or snow angels!

- Day 2. The theme for the second day is Penguins! I start class by reviewing key concepts from day 1 (safety, fitness, layering of clothing). The first activity today is the same scavenger hunt used on day 1, only this time with penguin-related items hidden in the snow. We keep the fun going with Penguin Relay Races and Snowy Puzzles (described on pages 35 and 36).

- Day 3. The theme for this day is Snowshoe Sports. Again, we lead off by reviewing key concepts (safety, fitness, layering) before getting into another scavenger hunt—this time using items related to winter sports. The class is then divided into three groups, each of which plays a different sport with snowshoes—baseball, football, or disc golf.

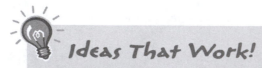

Ideas That Work!

H Share resources. Purchase one set of snowshoes that you can share with the other schools in your district. (Include money in your yearly budget to replace and repair the snowshoes.)

Buying, Using, and Storing Snowshoes

Of course, one early step in preparing a snowshoeing unit is to purchase snow-shoes! To research snowshoes and find general information about using them in physical education, visit the Winter Feels Good web page on the Snowlink website (www.snowlink.com/winterfeelsgoodhomepage.aspx). This site offers great information about how to incorporate snowshoeing into your program.

Ideally, you will be able to provide one pair of snowshoes for each student. Think about the largest class you teach and purchase five more than you need for that class so that you have some leeway if some shoes break. If this approach is not feasible for your budget, figure out how many pairs of snow-shoes you can afford and see where that leaves you. For example, if you can afford only enough snowshoes for half of your class, you will need to design your snowshoe lessons so that you have two activities going at the same time. That way, half the class can snowshoe while the other half does something else (e.g., builds snowpeople or makes snow angels). When designing your lesson in this way, you must consider the physical space for the two activities and make sure that you are able to supervise both of them. You cannot, for instance, send half your class out snowshoeing on a trail in the woods while the other half makes snowpeople. You would not be able to see both groups!

Your top priority when purchasing snowshoes for your physical education classes should be durability! The snowshoes must stand up to being repeat-edly put on and taken off by students in all of your classes. You know your students and how hard they can be on equipment. Make sure that the company you buy from understands how hard kids can be on the equipment and how limited your budget is. Put together a purchasing plan that includes repair and replacement. Talk to the company before you purchase your snowshoes

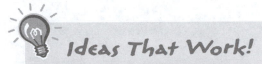

Ideas That Work!

T Inform your students and their families about websites that list places in your area where they can snowshoe! You can do this in your school's newsletter, on a handout, or on your school's own website. Consider giving extra credit to students who bring in information about relevant websites they have found. You can also highlight sites that calcu-late the calories burned while snowshoeing, such as FitDay (www.fitday.com/WebFit/ burned/calories_burned_Snow_shoeing. html) and Calorie Count (http://caloriecount. about.com/calories-burned-snow-shoeing-a567).

to find out the warranty plan and how much they will charge if you need to have snowshoes repaired. In addition, consider how often you will need to purchase new snowshoes and budget for it over the next 5 to 10 years.

I have found that Tubbs snowshoes (http://tubbssnowshoes.com) are the most durable snowshoes for use in physical education classes. I purchased Tubbs snowshoes 10 years ago and have had only 2 of the 35 pairs break. The 33 pairs of snowshoes we still have are going strong after 10 years of use by two different middle school programs!

It is very important to plan how you are going to store and transport your snowshoes. Look around at your school and see what your options are. For storage, I found an old closet that no one is using across from the gym and asked the maintenance staff to install hooks from which to hang the snowshoes when they are not in use. For transportation, I put two scooters under an old metal rack that someone was throwing out; I can put the shoes on the rack and wheel it around. Between classes, I keep the rack in a maintenance room that has a garage door and a floor drain (the drain is important because the snow on the shoes melts between classes and needs somewhere to go). This room is located right behind the locker rooms, which allows me to meet my students in the back hall, whereupon they come in and take their snowshoes off the rack. Then I open the garage door and we go out.

Courtesy of Sarah Fletcher.

This metal rack was on its way to the trash heap before it was rescued and made into a snowshoe transportation unit!

SNOWSHOEING LESSONS

Day 1: Enjoying the Great Outdoors

Get off on the right snowshoe by emphasizing proper equipment, safety, and fitness benefits. Then let the fun begin!

NASPE Standards

1, 3, 4, 5, 6

Equipment

- Examples of clothing to demonstrate layering principles
- Snowshoes (ideally, one pair per student)
- Pedometer for each student (or, if necessary, one for each pair of students, who can alternate days of using the pedometer)
- Scavenger hunt items (related to the theme of the great outdoors)
- Items for making snowpeople (e.g., carrots, scarves, items for eyes)

Fitness Goals

- Get outdoors and exercise. Students wear pedometers during the activity and aim to achieve a step count goal. You can either let them choose their own goal or designate a common goal for all students.
- Burn calories while snowshoeing. Let students know how many calories can be burned while snowshoeing.

Lesson Progression

1. Discuss the importance of layering clothing while exercising outdoors; give examples.
   - Wicking layer: Worn next to the skin, wicking garments should contain fibers that take moisture away from the skin and pass it on to the clothing fabric so that it can evaporate. Examples include thermal long underwear and long-sleeved T-shirts made of wicking material.
   - Insulating layer: This middle layer helps keep heat in and cold out. Examples include fleece, as well as cotton sweatshirts and sweaters.
   - Outside layer (weather protection): This layer guards against the elements (e.g., wind, snow, rain). It includes waterproof jackets, waterproof gloves, and hats.

2. Discuss equipment and safety. It's very important that students learn how to put on snowshoes quickly and securely so that time isn't wasted and so that they remain safe while wearing their snowshoes. Here is the best way I have found for my students to put on their own snowshoes with the least help (your instructions should contain no more than four steps!):

   1. Loosen the front and back straps of the snowshoe.
   2. Place the front of your foot into the snowshoe first.
   3. Secure the front and back straps tightly.
   4. Try out the fit of the snowshoe before you start.

Provide a rug or mat so that your students can practice putting on their snowshoes for the first time inside! The rug or mat keeps the snowshoes from sliding, and it is much easier to help students in the warmth of the building than outside in the cold!

Be sure to demonstrate proper removal as well.

To help students avoid wasting time, give them a meaningful motive for finishing the task. I use the Chilly Scavenger Hunt as an incentive for my students to put on their snowshoes quickly with the least amount of help from me. The sooner their shoes are on, the sooner we can play!

Designate an area each day where you will start and end class and hike back to that area.

3. Play Chilly Scavenger Hunt. During the hunt, the students locate hidden items after putting on their snowshoes as fast as they can so that they can start the hunt. The items should relate to today's lesson theme: the great outdoors!

4. Take a short hike around the area where you are snowshoeing and observe nature.

5. Old-Fashioned Fun: End the class by building snowpeople or making snow angels.

6. Hike back to where class started and take off the snowshoes.

Assessment

- Students check the number of steps on their pedometer.
- Students indicate their enjoyment of snowshoeing and getting outside by showing a quick thumbs-up or thumbs-down.

Students should know how to secure and remove their snowshoes properly and quickly!

CHILLY SCAVENGER HUNT

After teaching snowshoeing for 7 years, one problem I still faced was that of students taking too much time to put on their snowshoes. They would ask me for help, which wasted a lot of time. One day, I thought of hiding something out on the trail to motivate the students to get started. As I sat in my office planning my upcoming snowshoe unit, I saw out of the corner of my eye a green rubber chicken on one of my shelves. The light bulb went on, and the Chilly Scavenger Hunt was born! I now use this activity every day during this unit and have found that I hardly have to help anyone put on their snowshoes. The students literally start running as soon as they have their snowshoes on so they can find the hidden treasures!

- Before class starts, go out to the area where students will be snowshoeing and hide as many objects as possible. Suggestions include rubber chickens, poly spot shapes (e.g., penguins), and beanbag animals.
- When students come to class, explain that you have hidden (however many) objects in the area where they will be snowshoeing.
- Tell students that the faster they get their snowshoes on, the more time they will have to find as many objects as they can.
- When all of the students have their snowshoes on, follow the last student out and see how many objects have been found.
- When all of the objects have been found, the students hide the objects again for the next class.

Students love finding hidden objects in the Chilly Scavenger Hunt!

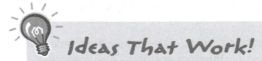

Ideas That Work!

H Get free equipment from your colleagues! Share with your teaching staff that you are collecting small items to use in your snowshoe scavenger hunt. You will probably receive a lot of great items!

NATURE HIKE

For this simple activity, take a short hike around the area where you are snowshoeing and observe nature. See if your students can name and categorize trees and birds. Discuss hibernation and which animals are hibernating at this time.

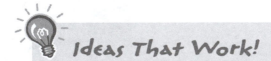

Ideas That Work!

H Ask science teachers to suggest science concepts that you can cover during your snowshoe nature walk that they are also covering in science class.

OLD-FASHIONED FUN

If the snow is good for packing, have your students make snow people. Take pictures of each snowperson that they build, then create a bulletin board in the gym to showcase the various snow people. You can also have students make snow angels.

Day 2: Penguins

Now that your students are a little more skilled with their snowshoes, they can spend some more time playing. Still, be sure to quickly review the same layering, safety, and equipment concepts from day 1 before getting started!

NASPE Standards

1, 3, 4, 5, 6

Equipment

- Pedometers
- Penguin-related items for the scavenger hunt
- Penguin-shaped poly spots for relay races
- Puzzles for the Snowy Puzzles activity (created and hidden ahead of time)

Fitness Goal

Students wear pedometers during the activity and aim to achieve a step count goal. You can either let students choose their own goal or designate a common goal for all students.

Lesson Progression

1. Review key concepts from day 1 (i.e., layering, safety, equipment).

2. Play Penguin Chilly Scavenger Hunt. This is basically the same hunt you played on day 1; just hide penguin-related items along the hiking trail for the students to find. The students need to put on their snowshoes as fast as they can so that they can start the scavenger hunt.

3. Play Penguin Relay Races. Use poly spots shaped like penguins as the objects for students to hand off to each other while participating in the races.

4. Play Snowy Puzzles. You can use pictures of today's theme or pictures of your students to create the puzzle pieces.

Assessment

- Students check the number of steps on their pedometer.
- Students indicate their enjoyment of snowshoeing and getting outside by showing a quick thumbs-up or thumbs-down.

PENGUIN RELAY RACES

Assign your students to relay teams of four members each before class starts and bring the team rosters with you. Give each team a penguin-shaped poly spot. Half the members of each team move down the field and face the other half of the team. The team member holding the penguin poly spot runs down the field to the first person in the other line and hands off the penguin. The new holder of the penguin runs back toward the other half of the team and hands it off to the next person—and so on, until everyone has run. The emphasis is not on winning but on having fun!

SNOWY PUZZLES

Before doing this activity, you'll need to make the puzzle pieces. You can use any picture you choose, but if you use pictures of your students the activity will be especially fun for them! During the first day of the snowshoeing unit, I group the students in fours and take pictures of each group while they are snowshoeing. At the end of that first day, I print all the pictures on regular computer paper, cut each picture into eight equal pieces, and glue the pieces to a piece of colored construction paper. Then laminate the puzzle pieces to make them more resilient. Make sure that all of the puzzles have the same number of pieces. If the puzzles have different numbers of pieces, it will drive you crazy trying to figure out how many pieces each group has to find! I keep a record of which color of construction paper I used for each group.

Before the first class of the day, set up cones around the outside of the area where you will hide the puzzle pieces. Next, hide the first class's puzzle pieces in the snow inside the coned area. Make sure that a small part of each puzzle piece shows above the snow so that the students can see it. Hide the pieces *only* in the coned area.

You can use any picture to make puzzle pieces!

Part of the buried puzzle pieces should be visible.

Set up colored cones (one for each group) at the starting point. If possible, use cones that match the colors of the puzzles.

Before starting the activity, ask your students to be careful of where they step when looking for puzzle pieces; it's easy to accidentally trample pieces down into the snow so that they cannot be found. To begin the activity, have two people at a time from each group go out and find one puzzle piece each, then run back and put the puzzle pieces on the ground next to their group's colored cone. Then the next two group members go out and look for two more pieces and bring them back. Students keep assembling the puzzle until it is finished.

When each group has found all of its puzzle pieces and assembled its puzzle on the ground, give the students the next class' puzzle pieces to hide in the coned area.

Day 3: Snowshoe Sports

Wearing snowshoes provides a way to add fun and novelty to common sports. It also exemplifies how creative thinking can show your students the limitless possibilities for lifetime fitness activity!

NASPE Standards

1, 3, 4, 5, 6

Equipment

- Pedometers
- Sport-related items to hide for the scavenger hunt
- Baseball: balls, bats, bases
- Football: balls, flags
- Flying discs

Fitness Goal

Students wear pedometers during the activity and aim to achieve a step count goal. You can either let students choose their own goal or designate a common goal for all students.

Lesson Progression

1. Review key concepts from days 1 and 2.

2. Play Sport Chilly Scavenger Hunt. Use items that correspond to the theme of winter sports or games.

3. Play snowshoe sports—baseball, football, and disc golf. Set up these three games before class. Once students are ready to play, arrange them into teams of four or fewer and assign each team to one of three groups (one group for each sport). For a small-sided baseball game, one person is the pitcher, two people play the infield, and one plays the outfield. Because it is cold the ball will not fly too far! For a small-sided football game, one person is the quarterback and the other three people go out for a pass. Players are not allowed to run at the quarterback or try to take their flag and the quarterback cannot run with the ball.

Assessment

- Students check the number of steps on their pedometer.
- Students indicate their enjoyment of snowshoeing and getting outside by showing a quick thumbs-up or thumbs-down.

Backpacking

These days, kids are spending more and more time indoors, where they are often focused on television, computers, or video games. As a result, many parents are looking for ways to get outside and enjoy nature with their children. What better way than going out for a short hike on a nature trail or in the woods with a backpack?

Backpacking can even provide a way for kids to enjoy technology in a heart-healthy way. The backpacking units that I teach include geocaching—a sort of scavenger hunt in which one uses a GPS (global positioning system) unit to find a hidden cache—for example, a small film canister with something hidden inside of it. Lots of kids who might otherwise be less than keen on getting outside and moving around will find that they can enjoy such activity when they are lured by gadgets and the thrill of adventure!

Unit Overview

I teach a 3-day backpacking unit, which I have found to be the perfect length for this unit. However, you could extend the unit a day by doing 2 days of geocaching.

- Day 1: Sizing It Up! On the first day, introduce students to the various types of backpacks available for hiking. Have your students try both external and internal frame packs and learn how to pack a backpack. Students then wear pedometers and go for a short hike while wearing one of the backpacks. During the hike, they learn the basics of how to use a compass, then proceed to use it to find their way back to the starting point of the hike.
- Day 2: The Heart of Hiking. Now that your students are familiar with the equipment, it's time to let them get to the heart of hiking! Students wear a pedometer and a heart rate monitor while hiking with their backpack. They participate in an activity (called How Fast Can You Hike?) that teaches them how to pace themselves while hiking.
- Day 3: Buried Treasure! This day is spent on learning the basics of geocaching, including how to use a GPS unit. Provide a GPS unit to each pair of students (or larger groups, if you do not have enough GPS units for pairs, though no more than four people per group). Take the students through the basic functions of the GPS unit that they will use for the day's geocaching lesson.

Equipment

If you do not have sufficient funding to purchase external and internal frame backpacks for your classes, you have several options. You might look for community sources who can help with funding; for example, perhaps a local hiking or outdoors group would be willing to help you purchase the backpacks. If it comes down to it, students can use their school backpacks. You also need a compass as well as items to put into the backpack (e.g., clothes, food, cooking items) to give the backpack a real-life weight and to provide an example of items necessary for a hike. Here, you might ask for donations from your school community. Additional needs include heart rate monitors, pedometers, and, for the geocaching activity, GPS units. Money for purchasing these items might be available through grants or a discount provided by a local sporting goods store.

It's important to ensure a proper backpack fit for all students.

BACKPACKING LESSONS

Day 1: Sizing It Up!

Students learn the differences between an internal- and external-frame backpack and how to measure their bodies to find the correct size of backpack. They also learn how to correctly pack their backpack and how to use a compass.

NASPE Standards

1, 3, 4, 5, 6

Equipment

- Compasses (ideally, one for every two students)
- Backpacks—external frame and internal frame (ideally, one backpack per student, but can be shared if necessary)
- Items to pack in backpacks (e.g., water bottles, clothing, small cookware)
- Pedometers (ideally, one per student, but can be shared by alternating days)

Fitness Goal

Students wear a pedometer while taking a hike with their backpack. They can predict how many steps they will take during the hike, then self-assess at the end of class by checking how many steps they actually took.

Lesson Progression

1. Show your students some examples of external-frame and internal-frame backpacks and discuss the benefits of each type. External-frame backpacks are best for heavy loads. They make it easy to access gear, are usually less expensive, require fewer adjustments, and hold the bulk of the pack away from the carrier's back, thus allowing air to circulate. Internal frame backpacks are best for balance because the load is held low and close to the body. These packs are best for off-trail hiking.

2. Teach your students how to measure for a correct fit. Discuss relevant body measurements. The carrier's height is not nearly as important as his or her torso length. Demonstrate the correct way to measure one's body for fitting a backpack. To measure torso length, you need help from a partner (students can pair up). The partner should measure along the spine from the seventh vertebra (the bump where the shoulder meets the neck) down to a point that is even with the top of the hip bones. This measured distance is the torso length.

3. Show your students how to pack a backpack. Lead them through the process. First, have them unpack their pack and go through what is in it. Discuss the items in the pack and their importance for hiking. Next, discuss how to pack the backpack correctly by placing the heaviest items on the bottom. When packing food, you need

Ideas That Work!

T Check the Internet or books on backpacking to learn about torso length and selecting a backpack size. You need to know which backpacks in your stockpile match certain torso lengths. JanSport is a great resource for backpacking information (www.jansport.com).

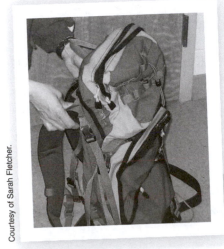

External-frame backpack.

Courtesy of Sarah Fletcher.

Internal-frame backpack.

Courtesy of Sarah Fletcher.

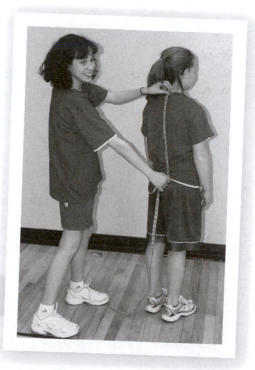

Students demonstrate measuring torso length.

to pack 2 pounds (about a kilogram) of food per day of hiking. You can usually lash a sleeping bag through loops located at the bottom of the backpack. Students then repack their backpack and take a short hike that ends back at school.

4. Show the students how to use a compass while hiking. End the class by having the students put the bearing on the compass that will lead them back to the school where the hike started, then have them use the compass while hiking back to school.

Assessment

- Students check their pedometers to see if each student reached the goal that he or she set at the start of class.
- Students do self-assessment of their use of a compass. They know they were successful if they end class in the area designated by the teacher.

Day 2: The Heart of Hiking

Your students now know how to select an appropriate backpack and how to pack it. Today, they wear a heart rate monitor and hike with their backpack.

NASPE Standards

1, 3, 4, 5, 6

Equipment and Facility

- Pedometers
- Heart rate monitors
- Handout: How Fast Can You Hike? (see figure 3.1, one copy per student)
- Backpacks
- 1-mile (1.6-kilometer) course (school track or a course set up by you before class)

Fitness Goals

At the beginning of class, students put on their pedometers and make an oral prediction of how many steps they will take today. Students also wear a heart rate monitor today but do not work out in a specific target heart rate zone. As an alternative to using heart rate monitors, you can have students take their pulse manually at their wrist or neck.

Lesson Progression

Students learn how to hike and pace themselves while wearing a heart rate monitor. They use the handout titled How Fast Can You Hike? (Alternatively, students can take their pulse manually at the neck or wrist at the end of each lap or at other determined spots along the course.) Students put on their selected backpack and go out to the designated course for the activity. I use a quarter-mile (0.4-kilometer) track. Instruct them to record their heart rate on the handout after each lap or at whatever interval makes sense for your track or course.

Assessment

- The student checks the pedometer to record how many steps he or she took during the hike and how close this total came to his or her predicted step count.
- The student records his or her heart rate on the handout as directed.

FIGURE 3.1 ▬▬▬▬▬▬

How Fast Can You Hike?

Name _____

Hiking all day with a loaded backpack is difficult. In the activity we are doing today, you will go outside and hike a course at a comfortable pace. You will wear a pedometer as well as a heart rate monitor to track your pulse in order to determine how fast you should hike. To conserve energy and be able to continue hiking for long periods, you should keep your pulse at 50 percent to 60 percent of your maximum.

Record your time, heart rate, and step count for each lap.

Lap 1   Time _____   Heart rate _____ Steps _____

Lap 2   Time _____   Heart rate _____ Steps _____

Lap 3   Time _____   Heart rate _____ Steps _____

Lap 4   Time _____   Heart rate _____ Steps _____

At this pace, how long would it take to hike 10 miles?

From C. Gorwitz, 2012, *Teaching healthy lifestyles in middle school PE: Strategies from an award-winning program* (Champaign, IL: Human Kinetics).

Day 3: Buried Treasure

Geocaching (scavenger hunting with a GPS unit) is a great lifetime activity to introduce to your students. For today's class, you take your students through the steps of using a GPS unit, and they practice using all of the buttons. To end the class, the students participate in an activity that I call Buried Treasure.

NASPE Standards

1, 3, 4, 5, 6

Equipment

- Pedometers
- Backpacks
- GPS units (labeled with identification numbers—for example, numbered 1 through 6 if you are hiding six plastic boxes for the buried treasure activity)
- Plastic boxes (labeled on top with identification numbers—for example, numbered 1 through 6 if you are using six GPS units)
- Small prizes to place inside each hidden plastic box (students each take a prize when their group finds a box)

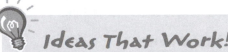

Ideas That Work!

H Talk to the science teachers at your school about working together to purchase GPS units that can be used in both science and physical education classes!

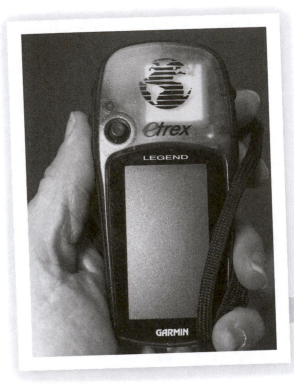

GPS unit.

Fitness Goal

At the start of class, set a class step goal of 3,000 and have students predict aloud how many steps they will take.

Lesson Progression

1. Describe to your students how to use a GPS unit. If you do not already know, ask for help at a local sporting goods store or use the Internet to find instructions.

2. Use the Buried Treasure activity to introduce students to geocaching. Direct students to the Official Global GPS Cache Hunt website (www.geocaching.com), where they can learn more about geocaching.

Assessment

- Students note the number of steps they took and compare it with the prediction they made.
- Students conduct a self-assessment of using GPS units. They know they were successful if they correctly locate their team's hidden plastic box.

BURIED TREASURE

Before class, draw a map of the area in which students are going to play the game. In class, arrange your students into groups (no more than six students in each group). I use six groups, but your division should be determined by your class size and the number of GPS units you have. Give each group a GPS unit that is labeled on the back with a number from 1 to 6 (or however many groups you use) and a blue plastic box labeled on top with the same number (and pre-stuffed with the prizes by the teacher).

Next, show your students how to use their GPS unit to mark their cache. The students then hide their cache (i.e., their blue box) and make sure to mark it exactly where it is hidden (if they are even one step off, it will not be marked correctly). After marking their caches, they bring back their GPS unit and show you on the map where they hid their cache so you can record its location. The group then switches its GPS unit with another group's unit and looks on the back of the new unit to see which numbered box they are looking for. The group members work to find the cache, whereupon each student takes a prize from inside the box, bring the GPS unit back to base, switch to a new GPS unit to find a new box, and continue in this manner until they have found all 6 caches.

Disc Golf

Disc golf can be taught to upper elementary, middle, and high school students, and it is a great lifetime activity to include in your physical education classes. It requires very little equipment, and all of your students can achieve success in playing it. If equipment limitations pose an obstacle, you can even use hula hoops and hula hoop holders and generic flying discs instead of metal Frisbee disc catchers and regulation Frisbee golf discs.

Disc golf offers many fitness benefits. Your students can wear pedometers or heart rate monitors to track the number of steps they take or record their heart rate while playing disc golf. Outside of class, students can improve their fitness by walking a 9- or 18-hole disc golf course. Family members can also benefit by walking the course with the student, which provides a time for families to grow closer by talking with each other while playing the game.

Unit Overview

- Day 1: Discs Take Flight! The objective for day 1 is skill work (i.e., getting discs in the air). Introduce the skill of throwing a disc into the wind and have your students take time to practice with a partner. One effective way to introduce and practice disc-throwing skills involves a simple lead-up game called How Low Can You Go? Students can also practice by participating in a driving range activity. To assess your students' fitness levels, set a step count goal and have them wear pedometers during class.

- Day 2: Rules of Play. This day you address three issues: disc golf rules of etiquette, skill assessment (to improve student learning), and game play. Students are assessed using the disc golf rubric (see page 50). You can have students use the skills they learned on day 1 by playing a fun disc golf game called Spray-Paint Golf (with hazards that are spray-painted different colors). Fitness is stressed by using pedometers and a class step-count goal.

■ Day 3: Goofy Golf Scramble. Today's goals are to have fun and improve fitness. Students have fun by playing the Goofy Golf Scramble, which involves doing activities at each hole (e.g., knocking a rubber chicken off of the disc catcher). Fitness is addressed by having students wear pedometers and take as many steps as possible while playing in the scramble.

Equipment

Equipment for your disc golf unit can vary with your budget. Ideally, you can obtain nine metal disc catchers; much like the holes in regular golf, the catchers are placed at the end of each hole, and the player's disc must land inside the catcher in order to finish the hole. Of course, you also need flying discs (one for each student) and pedometers. If your budget is restrictive, you can use hula hoops and hula hoop holders instead of disc catchers and generic flying discs instead of regulation Frisbee golf discs.

Disc catcher.

DISC GOLF LESSONS

Day 1: Take Flight!

Let the disc flying begin! On this first day, teach your students the proper technique for throwing a golf disc. Have students emphasize fitness as well by wearing a pedometer and working to meet the class' daily step count goal.

NASPE Standards

1, 2, 4, 5

Equipment

- Six large cones with attached markers to indicate distance
- One flying disc for each pair of students
- One small cone for each pair of students
- One pedometer for each student

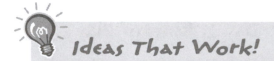

Ideas That Work!

A I have my students write down their predictions for the number of steps they will take on the disc golf course. The students really like to use prediction, and it motivates them to move out on the course (I set a minimum number of steps for predictions so that they can't predict a really low step count!).

Fitness Goal

Students wear pedometers while practicing the skills of throwing a flying disc. At the beginning of class, they predict how many steps they will take today, and after doing the activity they check their pedometer to see if they met the prediction they made.

Lesson Progression

1. Teach disc-throwing skills. Emphasize throwing the disc low so that it will go farther. Students also need to realize that when playing disc golf outside, wind is a factor. One effective way to introduce and practice throwing skills is to play a simple game that I call How Low Can You Go? Each pair of partners has one disc and two small cones. The partners stand facing one another, and each has a cone just in front of his or her feet.

The partners take turns throwing the disc low, aiming for the small cone in front of the other person's feet. Start the partners out about two giant steps from one another, then signal them at intervals to move farther apart.

2. Set up a driving range so that students can practice throwing the disc for distance. The disc driving range is exactly like a golf driving range except that it involves flying discs instead of clubs and balls. In order to do this activity, you need a large area (I use the football practice field for my driving range). Before class starts, set up cones with attached distance markers: 25 yards (or meters), 50 yards, and so on. Use an agreed-upon signal to start everyone at the same time (I use a whistle). Everyone should wear a pedometer (they'll accumulate a lot of steps in this activity!), and each student should have a partner. One partner throws the disc, and the other marks where the disc lands. On the first whistle, the partner with the disc throws it as hard as he or she can. On the second whistle, the other partner runs out and stands where the disc landed.

Assessment

- Students check the number of steps on their pedometer and compare the result with their prediction.
- Students assess how far they can throw the disc simply by participating in the driving range activity, seeing how far their disc flew through the air, and noting the distance marked by their partner.

Day 2: Rules of Play

Now that students know how to properly throw a disc, they need to know the rules of play. Teach them the rules and the appropriate etiquette and have them practice their skills in a game of Spray-Paint Golf.

NASPE Standards

1, 2, 4, 5, 6

Equipment

- Disc golf rules quiz (can be done on your teacher web page)
- Disc golf rubric
- Pencils for each group (to record their disc golf scores and step counts)
- Pedometers (one per student)
- Flying discs
- Cone
- Disc catchers (or hula hoops and hula hoop holders)
- Course map and scorecard

Fitness Goal

At the start of class, each student predicts how many steps he or she will take today during class. At the end of class, students check their pedometers to see if their prediction was accurate. If you also set a classwide step count goal, students will check their pedometers to see if they achieved this goal.

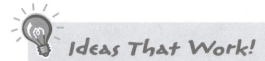

Ideas That Work!

T You can use technology to help your students learn the rules of disc golf! You can include a section on your physical education website that lists disc golf rules and contains a quiz, then assign your students to go to the site and take the quiz. You can either require the students to print their quiz and turn it in for the written work portion of their physical education grade or have them e-mail it to you and save paper!

Lesson Progression

1. Disc golf rules and etiquette. Go over the rules of etiquette for disc golf. Each player must stay at the tee box (the start of each disc golf hole) until all players have made their first throw. For subsequent throws, the person whose disc is farthest from the hole always throws first. Everyone playing together must stay behind the person who is throwing.

2. Spray-Paint Golf. For this game, you create a disc golf course with spray-painted hazards (e.g., a water hazard would be spray-painted onto the grass using blue paint, and the word water would be spray-painted inside). The objective of the game is for students to keep their disc from landing inside the spray-painted hazards.

3. Online disc golf quiz. You can integrate technology by putting a disc golf rules quiz online. Instruct students to take the quiz before the next class (either for fun or for a grade).

Assessment

Use the disc golf rubric (see figure 3.2 on page 50) to assess your students' skills, knowledge, and play during the class period.

SPRAY-PAINT GOLF

The day before playing Spray-Paint Golf, create a disc golf course in a large outdoor area. Use colored cones to mark tee boxes and the corresponding disc catchers—or if you are using a hula hoop instead of a catcher, put the cone inside the hoop. This setup helps students identify each hole's location and makes it easy to determine where each group will start playing.

Draw a simple map of the course that shows holes and hazards. Leave room at the bottom of the map for a golf scorecard that lists par for each hole. Give one copy of the map to each group.

FIGURE 3.2

Disc Golf Rubric

Name _____

Skill assessed	Advanced	Proficient	Basic	
Throw—NASPE standards 1 and 2	3 points	2 points	1 point	
Backhand and fore-hand	Steps with correct foot (i.e., the foot on the same side as the throwing arm).	Steps with correct foot (i.e., the foot on the same side as the throwing arm) 80 percent of the time.	No step at all.	
	Flicks wrist.	Flicks wrist.	Does not flick wrist.	
	Disc flies parallel to the ground.	Disc flies at an angle to the ground.	Disc flies for short distance and either curves or wobbles.	
			TOTAL	
Knowledge of disc golf—NASPE standard 5	3 points	2 points	1 point	
Good sporting behavior	Follows all rules of disc golf.	Follows the rules at half of the holes.	Doesn't follow the rules of disc golf.	
	Waits at tee box for all players to throw.	Waits at the tee box at half of the holes.	Never waits at the tee box. Throws the disc into the group playing in front of him or her.	
	Always waits for the player whose disc is farthest from hole to throw.	Sometimes waits for the player whose disc is farthest from hole to go first.	Never follows rules of disc golf etiquette.	
	Yells "Fore!" if the disc is coming.	Yells "Fore!" half of the time.	Never yells "Fore!" Throws into the group playing front of him or her.	
			TOTAL	
Game play and fit-ness—NASPE stan-dards 3, 4, and 6	6 points	3 points	1 point	
	Takes his or her turn.	Doesn't always take his or her turn.	Never takes his or her turn—just throws the disc whenever he or she wants to.	
	Jogs to each hole.	Walks to each hole.	Moves very slowly to each hole.	
	Knows how to keep score and what his or her score is. Helps others with scoring.	Knows how to keep score.	Doesn't know the score.	
Pedometer steps	3,000 or more	2,999–2,000	2,000 or fewer	
			TOTAL	
			TOTAL SCORE	

From C. Gorwitz, 2012, *Teaching healthy lifestyles in middle school PE: Strategies from an award-winning program* (Champaign, IL: Human Kinetics).

Cones may be used (A) on the ground or (B) on top of a disc catcher to help students identify each hole's location from a distance.

Before play begins, agree with students on the signal you will use to mark the start of play. I have my students run out to their assigned starting hole and wait for my whistle. When they hear the whistle, they can begin playing.

I use a shotgun start, in which each group is assigned a hole to start on. Group 1 starts at hole 1, group 2 starts at hole 2, and so on. All of the students tee off (i.e., make their first throw) simultaneously to start play.

Spray-Paint Golf is generally played like regular disc golf. Each student throws his or her disc, runs to wherever it lands, makes the next throw, and continues in this manner until the disc lands in the disc catcher. The difference lies in the presence of the hazards, which add one penalty stroke to a student's score if not avoided and require students to throw the disc properly and allow for effective skill assessment.

Day 3: Goofy Golf Scramble

To pique your students' interest on day 3 of the unit, have them play the Goofy Golf Scramble, in which each hole requires them to try a goofy skill!

NASPE Standards
1, 3, 4, 5, 6

Equipment
- Pedometers (one per student)
- Disc golf rubric
- Colored cones to mark the start of each hole
- Pencils for each group (to record their scores and step counts)
- Goofy Golf scorecard (see figure 3.3)
- Flying discs (ideally, one per student)
- Goofy Golf items for each hole (e.g., rubber chicken, colored cone, shark-shaped poly spot, pinwheel)

Fitness Goal
At the start of class, each student predicts how many steps he or she will take today during class. You can also set a classwide step count goal. At the end of each hole, students record their step count. At the end of class, they total their steps taken during all nine holes and see if they achieved the class step goal that you set.

Lesson Progression
The Goofy Golf Scramble is the day's only activity. Students have fun practicing their skills, all while racking up pedometer steps!

Assessment
Use the Disc Golf Rubric to assess students' skills and game play. Students will also be assessed on the basis of their Goofy Golf scorecard; they are graded on filling out the card correctly and on the number of steps taken.

GOOFY GOLF SCRAMBLE

Before class, set up each hole of the Goofy Golf Scramble. Use a colored cone at the start of each hole. For the scramble, use a shotgun start and assign each student group a hole to start with. Create a goofy theme for each hole. Here are some examples:

- Chicken Knockout. Place a rubber chicken on top of the disc catcher. The first student to knock it off gets to subtract two strokes from his or her score.

FIGURE 3.3

Goofy Golf Scorecard

Player	Hole 1: Chicken Knockout— par 5	Hole 2: Longest Drive—par 4	Hole 3: Blind Drive (Close Your Eyes)—par 3	Hole 4: Under-the-Leg Putt— par 4	Hole 5: Shark Attack— par 5	Hole 6: Regular Play—par 4	Total
Susie	6	4	5	6	6	5	32
	800 steps	300 steps	750 steps	300 steps	700 steps	350 steps	3,200 steps
Juan							
Rita							
Jerome							

From C. Gorwitz, 2012, *Teaching healthy lifestyles in middle school PE: Strategies from an award-winning program* (Champaign, IL: Human Kinetics).

- Longest Drive. Place a cone at the beginning of this hole. The student with the longest drive in each group moves the colored cone to where his or her drive landed. At the end of the round, leave some time and have the class go back to that hole and see who had the longest drive in the class.
- Blind Drive. Students close their eyes while throwing their first drive.
- Under-the-Leg Putt. When students get close to the hole, they have to throw the disc under a leg.
- Shark Attack. Place shark-shaped poly spots around the hole and put up a sign that says, "Beware of sharks!"

Assign the students into nine groups (if you are playing a nine-hole course). Have each group go out to its colored cone to start the scramble and then proceed to play all nine holes. Students keep score by using the Goofy Golf scorecard and record their step counts for each hole. When they have gone through the whole course, they total their golf score and step count.

Summary

After looking over the lifetime activities I have described for you in this chapter, start thinking of one lifetime activity you can add to your physical education curriculum. Do you feel confident in using one of the three activities described for you here, or is there another activity that comes to mind? You can use the following questions to help you create the lifetime activity that fits for your classes.

Challenge Questions

P What is the first lifetime activity that you are going to plan? What equipment do you already have that you can use in planning this activity? What equipment would you need to purchase in order to teach the activity?

A What teaching strategies are needed for this lifetime lesson so that at least 50 percent of class time is spent in doing moderate or vigorous activity? What skills do students need in order to be successful in learning this lifetime activity?

T How can you include heart rate monitors or pedometers in this lifetime activity lesson? Can any apps for electronic devices be used to enhance the lesson?

H Is anyone in your community an expert at one of the lifetime activities that you plan to teach? Might that person come to your class to assist you? Could anyone on your teaching staff help you teach this lifetime activity? Might information related to this lifetime activity be included in any other subject matter?

chapter 4

Fitness Warm-Ups

Use the five components of fitness to plan fun warm-up activities that build your students' bodies and minds!

In many PE classes, the first 10 minutes are wasted with roll call, sitting in squads, or even aimless goofing around. You can take back that time and give your students the gift of increased knowledge and better health by planning warm-ups that are ready for them to do as soon as they enter your class. Structuring these warm-ups to incorporate the five components of fitness—cardiorespiratory endurance, muscular strength, muscular endurance, flexibility, and body composition and nutrition—is an easy way to emphasize healthy lifestyles in your curriculum throughout the year.

Approach the PATH . . .

P You can streamline your organizational process and enjoy high-quality lesson **planning** if you dedicate 1 week per month to a specific component of fitness. Advance planning also gives you the time you need in order to plan warm-ups that kids really love! When students come to class, their first question is always, "What are we doing today?" To answer that question, I write the key fitness component for the week on a dry-erase board placed in the locker room; I also note the name of the warm-up activity for the day. Another way to get your students excited about fitness is to designate 1 week per semester when the students are in charge of planning the fitness-related warm-up activities. Students use many skills in planning these activities—for example, problem solving, teamwork, and creativity—and the activities they create provide you with great warm-up options for use in future classes!

A One of the main goals of teaching physical education is planning lessons that let students spend at least 50 percent of their class time doing moderate or vigorous **activity**. You are well on your way to achieving this goal when you start your students into a fitness-related warm-up activity as soon as they set foot in your class! The fitness activities presented in this chapter provide not only a spark to improve your students' fitness but also key information about how to lead a healthy lifestyle.

T You can spice up your fitness-focused warm-ups by using appropriate **technology**, including software apps, pedometers, and heart rate monitors. You and your students can easily use apps that provide instant feedback about heart rate and other key fitness information. Pedometers enable you and your students to track the steps they accumulate toward meeting a step count goal set for the day's class. Using an online calendar can help you map out each week's five components of fitness activities.

H Structuring warm-up activities to address the five components of fitness allows you to integrate science, math, language arts, and health in a learning experience marked by **harmony**. For example, students can write journal entries about the fitness topic of the day and reflect on how they might apply what they have learned to their everyday lives. An example fitness topic could be TV commercial push-ups. Students' write about how doing five push-ups instead of watching the commercials can improve muscular strength. Warm-up time can also include math problems and science concepts. The sky is the limit when you think outside the box to get creative about the weekly fitness component!

Emphasizing Fitness Components

The five components of fitness should form an integral part of your physical education program. The following are some benefits of using this approach:

- Teaches students what it means to be fit (fitness concepts)
- Creates many opportunities for cross-curricular activities (e.g., nutrition education) that enhance learning across the curriculum
- Offers you a template for creating a wide variety of fun and creative programming

For all these reasons, when our school district won a 2001 PEP grant, the three teachers who wrote the grant (Marcia Schmidt, Cheryl Richardson, and I) made the five components of fitness an integral part of our program. At the middle school level, I highlighted one or two components of fitness in our warm-ups during each week. The first week of the month emphasized cardiorespiratory endurance, the second week addressed muscular strength and muscular endurance, the third week covered flexibility, and the fourth week highlighted body composition and nutrition.

I start planning the five-components-of-fitness activities by making a list of everything I want my students be able to use outside my class in order to lead a healthy lifestyle:

- Vocabulary
- Fitness concepts
- Nutrition information
- Healthy lifestyle examples
- Strategies

This information guides me in choosing fitness-related warm-ups and other activities. I devote the first 5 to 10 minutes of each class to a warm-up activity addressing the week's featured fitness component. On Fridays, my students do an activity called Fitness Friday (see page 76 for an example of the Fitness Friday Exercise Card) that is linked to the key fitness component for the week. For example, during muscular strength week the students do a muscular strength activity after they finish their heart rate monitor workout (which always serves as the first Fitness Friday activity, since cardiorespiratory fitness is not only emphasized 1 week per month but is also built into the other components of fitness wherever appropriate). I gauge my students' knowledge of these important fitness concepts by means of two assessments, which are discussed further in the final section of this chapter.

By concentrating on one component of fitness during each week, students develop a better sense of each component and how they can apply it to their everyday lives. They also learn the importance of being physically fit and begin to understand that it takes knowledge and exercise in all of the components to be healthy.

Using Apps to Teach the Five Components of Fitness

Students today use technology in every facet of their lives, and physical education class is no exception! Two awesome yet simple apps that I use in my classes are iHeartRate and iMuscle (both available in the Apple iTunes store). The iHeartRate app lets you take your pulse at your neck and use your other hand to tap with your finger on the screen to show your current heart rate. The iMuscle app shows students which muscles are used while performing various skills. These are only two examples—many more fitness apps are available for use in physical education. Apps can provide a great way for you to motivate your students to exercise outside of class time. For example, you can have your students use an app while exercising, save the data, and bring it to class the next day for you to review. Students can also use the pedometer app to see if they are reaching the goal of 10,000 steps a day. They can share in class how many steps they took during the previous day, and if they did not meet the goal, you can give them suggestions for integrating more fitness time into their schedules.

I would recommend starting with just one app and using it at home before you use it in your classroom. After you feel comfortable using it, share it with your students! If you are already using apps in your everyday life, share them with your students and talk about how the app is helping you lead a healthy lifestyle. You can also challenge your students to bring in titles of fitness or healthy lifestyle apps to class for you to check out. It is not necessary for the students to purchase the app—they can simply be in charge of researching what is available, and you can include money in your budget to purchase apps and try them out with your students to get their feedback. You will be amazed at how excited your students get about fitness when you start including apps in your lessons!

Cardiorespiratory Fitness Warm-Ups

Cardiorespiratory fitness involves the body's ability to perform large-muscle exercise over a prolonged period at moderate or high intensity; thus it is an important part of an overall fitness program. The following activity examples are quick and easy to set up, and they will help your students improve their cardiorespiratory fitness and start leading a healthier lifestyle.

FROGS AND TURTLES

Equipment

- Frog-shaped and turtle-shaped beanbags (one set of each primary color of frog and turtle for each group of students in your class; alternative option—laminated index cards with pictures of different-colored frogs and turtles)
- One hula hoop per group
- One hula hoop in the center of the playing area to hold all of the colored beanbag animals
- Equipment in each group's hula hoop (one jump rope, one large exercise ball)
- Laminated frog posters and turtle posters (one of each for every group in your class; examples shown on page 60)

Preparation

1. Create frog and turtle posters (see figure 4.1 on page 60). Each group needs one frog poster and one turtle poster.
2. Place one hula hoop on the floor in front of each group around the outside of a coned area that is about the size of a regulation basketball court. Inside each hula hoop, place one jump rope and one large exercise ball; beside each hoop, place a turtle poster and a frog poster.
3. Put a hula hoop in the center of the coned area and place the colored frogs and turtles inside the hoop.

Description

1. Divide the class into groups of no more than four students each and assign a hula hoop to each group.
2. Ask the class which is faster—a frog or a turtle? Students will answer that a frog is faster. Explain that the frog represents a cardiorespiratory endurance activity and that the turtle, since it is slower, represents a muscular strength activity.
3. Explain that each group starts by sending one person to the middle hoop to select a colored frog and bring it back to the group. The group members then find the exercise on the frog poster that corresponds to the color of their frog and do that exercise.
4. Next, another student from each group returns the frog to the middle hoop and brings a colored turtle to the group. As before, the students find the corresponding color (this time in turtle form) on the poster and do that exercise.
5. The group repeats this process, alternating frogs and turtles, until they have chosen one animal of each color and done the corresponding exercise for each.

FIGURE 4.1A

Frog Poster

- Red frog—Jog 2 laps around the coned area.

- Yellow frog—Everyone in your group holds onto one jump rope and jogs together once around the coned area.

- Blue frog—Run in place for 20 steps with your arms held out straight in front of you. Lift your knees high so that they hit your hands. Count out loud to 20.

- Green frog—Your group forms a circle, and everyone performs 20 jumping jacks while counting them aloud. Say each number louder than the one before!

- Purple frog—Gallop twice around the coned area.

- Orange frog—Grapevine-step once around the coned area.

From C. Gorwitz, 2012, *Teaching healthy lifestyles in middle school PE: Strategies from an award-winning program* (Champaign, IL: Human Kinetics).

FIGURE 4.1B

Turtle Poster

- Red turtle—Put the hula hoop on the floor. Each group member gets into the push-up position with his or her hands on the outside of the hula-hoop. Walk both hands inside of the hoop, then back out. Do this 20 times.

- Yellow turtle—Lunge walk: Do 6 lunges, walking forward, with your hands on your hips. Then do 6 lunges walking backward.

- Blue turtle—Your group sits down and forms a circle with feet hooked together. Everyone does curl-ups and sings the song "Row, Row, Row Your Boat." Repeat three times, getting louder each time!

- Green turtle—Wall sit: Sing the ABC song as loudly as you can while holding the wall-sit position.

- Purple turtle—Everyone does 5 push-ups using the large exercise ball.

- Orange turtle—All group members hold onto the hula hoop and slide clockwise 10 times while counting aloud. Then go counterclockwise and count out loud 10 times!

From C. Gorwitz, 2012, *Teaching healthy lifestyles in middle school PE: Strategies from an award-winning program* (Champaign, IL: Human Kinetics).

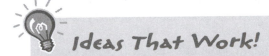

Ideas That Work!

A No standing in line! Whenever your students are doing an activity, have those who are waiting for their turn do an exercise or mini-activity while they wait. Incorporate movement at all times! Think of various ways to set up the activity so that there is no standing around (e.g., create several groups and provide enough equipment so that no one has to share or have laminated index cards with lists of exercises on them for students to do while waiting their turn).

HIGH-FLYING FITNESS

Equipment

- Colored flying discs (red, blue, green, orange)
- Cones (with colors that match the discs, if possible)
- High-flying fitness cards made with index cards and colored markers (one per student)

Preparation

1. Before class starts, divide the class into groups—red, blue, green, and orange—of no more than four students each. Depending on the size of your class you might need to have at least two games going on at once. If that is the case, you will need to have two groups of each color.

2. Create the high-flying fitness cards. Laminate them so that they can be used many times! Use colored markers to write the information on each index card. Each color (group) should have a theme; for example, blue cards could all be related to the theme of rewarding oneself for healthy eating. You would use a blue marker to write an example of good rewards on each card. Pick themes related to concepts you want to reinforce!

3. Create a colored poster for each group. Use colored construction paper that matches the colors of the groups and label each poster with the group's theme. For example, use a blue piece of paper and write "Rewarding Yourself for Healthy Eating" on it. Put

the posters at various spots on the wall. At the end of the activity, students gather near these posters, and you ask each group which category their cards belong in and to explain why.

4. Set up a cone to mark a home base for each group. Place the cones outside of a large area (e.g., basketball court). The cones can be matched to their group color, though this is not necessary. Place the flying disc that matches each group's color by the cone, then put the high-flying fitness cards in the middle of the activity area, equidistant from the groups' home bases, so that no group gains the advantage of running a shorter distance to reach the cards.

Description

1. Instruct the members of each group to form a line behind their cone. Let them know that when play begins, one group member will pick up the group's colored disc while another will go out to the middle of the activity area (by the high-flying fitness cards) to receive the flying disc when it is thrown.

2. Inform each group that the students waiting in line will do an exercise while waiting for their turn (you can hold up cards with exercises on them or post a list of exercises for students to do).

3. Explain that the person holding the disc will throw it to the group member who is waiting by the cards. The person in the middle will catch the disc, then pick up one of his or her team's index cards with the group's color (e.g., members of the red team will pick up the index card with the red writing on it), run back to the group, and hand the disc to the next person in line. Meanwhile the person who threw the disc runs to the middle and prepares to catch the disc, pick up an index card, run back to the group, and hand the disc to the next person in line. Group members proceed in this manner until they have obtained all of their colored cards. Everyone in line is still doing an activity while they wait.

4. Next, instruct the members to get together as a group beside their group's colored poster and discuss what category their colored cards match up with and why their cards match that category.

5. Go to each group and have them hold up their colored cards and explain to the entire class which category their cards match up with and why. Ask the students to make connections to things they do in their personal lives!

WORD WALL FITNESS

Equipment

- One poster board (for each grade level taught)
- Markers
- Exercise equipment (if any) for activities chosen as rewards

Preparation

1. At the beginning of the school year, create a list of five to eight healthy vocabulary terms at each grade level. These terms should be important ones for your students to learn in order to lead a healthy lifestyle; for example, you might use the word *elasticity* when covering the concept of flexibility. You can use the list for this particular activity and throughout the school year when teaching about living a healthy lifestyle.

2. Select one of the key terms for each grade level. Here are examples for the topic of cardiorespiratory endurance: *breathing rate* (sixth grade), *pulse rate* (seventh grade), and *aerobic capacity* (eighth grade). Write the chosen term on a piece of poster board but leave out some of the letters. For example, when using the sixth-grade term *(breathing rate),* you might write the following: b r _ _ t _ i _ g _ a _ e. Put the poster board on the wall (or, if you are outside, simply hold it up).

Description

1. Point out the poster showing the key term and explain the area of fitness to which it relates. Have students guess one consonant at a time to fill in the missing letters of the word.

2. If students want to purchase a vowel, they get to reward their bodies with exercise! For example, you might have students do 10 push-ups or sit-ups for every vowel purchased.

3. If students get a letter right, fill it in on the poster. Keep going until the students have guessed the term.

4. When students have guessed the term correctly, ask them to define the term and use it in a sentence.

5. Have your students wear pedometers for this activity. You can use them in several different ways. You can have the numbers of your pedometers in a hat and pull out one number. The student whose pedometer corresponds with that number will be the first person to guess a letter for the term. You can also have students predict (as a class or individually) how many steps they will take during class and write it on the key term poster. At the end of class, see how accurate the students' predictions were!

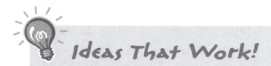

Ideas That Work!

H Create a space in your gym for a Word Wall. Many groups probably use your gym, and the Word Wall enables them to see the words that students are learning in your classes. If you don't have a gymnasium, you can find a place somewhere in your school to put up your word wall. You can refer back to the word wall at any time during your classes when students have questions!

WIPE OUT HEART DISEASE!

Equipment

- Volleyballs (ideally, one for every two students; at least one for every four students)
- Music player and recording of the song "Wipe Out"
- Posters listing risk factors for heart disease

Preparation

1. Make one poster for each heart disease risk factor (e.g., high-fat diet, obesity, high cholesterol, inactivity, smoking).
2. Before the activity starts, discuss the risk factors with your students.

Description

1. Have students pair up with a partner.
2. Tell students that when the music starts, they should start jogging anywhere in the activity area. The partners take turns carrying a ball while they move in space.
3. When the drum solo starts, the students find their partners and pass the ball back and forth while you hold up a card listing a risk factor for heart disease (e.g., inactivity). The students shout out examples of that risk factor while passing the ball with their partner (e.g., watching TV, playing video games).
4. Continue in this manner through the end of the song.

Muscular Strength Warm-Ups

Muscular strength is the ability of a muscle group or groups to exert maximal force. The activities listed in this section are quick and can be set up easily in any area. The teacher should allow about eight to ten minutes for this warm-up activity.

PLANK OR WALL SIT

Equipment

Stopwatch or other timing device

Preparation

1. Before doing this activity, teach your students the correct form for doing the plank (i.e., a push-up position with the forearms on the floor). Use specific cue words such as "forearms touching the floor" and "toes curled under."
2. Include time to practice doing the plank in warm-up periods prior to doing this activity.

Description

1. Have each student find a space on the floor and lie down on his or her stomach.
2. Give verbal cues about how to perform the plank—for example: "Place your forearms on the floor and clasp your hands together. Curl your toes under and push your body up into a push-up position, but instead of using your hands, keep your forearms on the ground."
3. Give students a short time to practice the plank.
4. Instruct students that when they can no longer hold the plank position, they should let their stomach come down to the floor.
5. Give the students an agreed-upon cue (e.g., whistle blow or the word *go*) to begin performing the plank and then hold it as long as they can.
6. Run the stopwatch until the last student has stopped holding the plank position.

Emphasize correct technique for the plank position: forearms touching the ground and toes curled under.

MATH PUSH-UPS

Equipment

- One set of dice (purchased or made by covering a small shoebox with brown paper bag material and marking numbers on it)
- Index cards (one set of cards for each set of partners)
- Alternative: laminated index cards listing math problems and taped to the boxes

Preparation

1. Before class starts, prepare the dice and the index cards listing the math problems to be used.
2. You can talk with your school's math teachers at each grade level to find out what they are covering in their math classes and cover that same material in your physical education class.
3. One die should have the math concept words on each side of the die (e.g., addition, subtraction, multiplication). The other die should have numbers or math problems with a space between the numbers to insert the math concept that is rolled on the other die.

Description

1. At the beginning of class, have your students use locomotor movements to move around in general space.
2. Prompt the students to find a partner who likes the same type of ice cream. This is just one example of a creative way to find a partner; another option would be to find someone born in the same month. No doubt you will think of others.
3. Have one partner in each pair get a pair of dice and an index card naming a math problem concept (e.g., multiplication, addition, subtraction). That partner places the card faceup between the two partners and places the dice where both partners can reach them.
4. On your signal (e.g., a whistle blow or a certain word), the students perform one push-up, then roll the dice and use the math concept card to solve the problem.
5. Repeat this process for 3 to 5 minutes.

ROLLING YOUR WAY TO FITNESS

Equipment

- Digital camera with which to take pictures of students performing strength activities
- Cube with plastic sides that open so you can insert a picture (alternative: picture cube made by taping pictures to a small shoebox)

Preparation

1. Before class begins, take pictures of your students performing the strength activities that you determine are most important for them.
2. Print the pictures and slide them into (or tape them onto) the cube. Change the pictures each time you do this activity.

Description

1. Students move in general space by performing a locomotor activity designated by you.
2. Using a whistle blow or cue word, signal the students to stop and find a partner with whom they share something particular in common (e.g., favorite color, birthday month, favorite ice cream flavor).

3. Randomly pick one set of partners to come up and roll the cube that shows the strength activity pictures.

4. Have the students who rolled the die demonstrate the strength activity indicated by the result of the roll. Then have everyone in class perform the activity.

5. Next, have the students return to moving in open space (doing a different loco-motor activity), then give the cue to stop again and repeat steps 3 and 4. Continue for approximately 5 minutes.

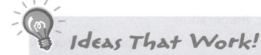

Ideas That Work!

P Glue the pictures you take for this activity onto colored pieces of construction paper and laminate them so that you can use them again and again!

You can use written exercise instructions or pictures in the cube.

Wall Sit
Hold For 20 Seconds

SPOT STRENGTH

Equipment

- Poly spots (or computer mouse pads, perhaps donated by a local business that no longer uses them)
- Index cards showing pictures of students doing strength activities (one per poly spot or mouse pad)
- Music

Preparation

1. Put names and pictures of your students doing various strength activities on large index cards (e.g., push-up, exercise ball sit-up, biceps curl). The activities can be repeated on the cards; for example, the biceps curl could be listed on three cards.
2. Laminate the cards and attach them to the poly spots or mouse pads, one picture per spot or pad.
3. Place the poly spots or pads with pictures throughout the activity area.

Description

1. Begin the class with a short discussion about the importance of breathing correctly while performing each strength activity. Explain that students should exhale during the hardest part of the strength activity.
2. Start the music and give your students a bit of time to jog around the activity area and look at the spots and attached pictures.
3. Stop the music and have the students come back to you, then give them the following instructions: When the music starts, go stand by a spot (if your class is very large, students can share the spots) and perform the pictured strength activity. When the music stops, move to another spot and start another strength activity when the music restarts. (Stop the music about every 30 seconds.)
4. Repeat steps 2 and 3 for approximately 3 minutes.

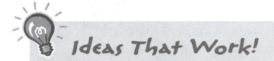

Ideas That Work!

A You can motivate your students by informing them that you are looking for individuals to perform the strength activities on video as an example for other students to follow. This invitation encourages students to practice hard and execute the activities correctly (and even practice on their own) so that they can be videorecorded while doing the activities.

Flexibility Warm-Ups

Oftentimes, flexibility does not receive as much attention as it should in physical education. I devote the same amount of warm-up time to flexibility as I do to muscular strength and cardiorespiratory endurance. To start, share your definition of flexibility with your students. Here is the definition that I use: Flexibility is the ability to move joints or muscles through their full range of motion.

CARDIO YOGA

Equipment

- Colored construction paper
- Photographs of students doing yoga poses (enough for students to use in groups of no more than three; number of poses determined by class size)
- Yoga mats (one per pair of students)
- High-energy music

Preparation

1. Take pictures of students doing each yoga pose. Print the pictures and glue them onto colored pieces of construction paper.
2. Spread out the yoga picture cards (facedown) in the middle of the chosen activity area (e.g., the center circle on a basketball court).
3. Spread out the yoga mats in a large rectangle located outside of the center area that contains the yoga picture cards.

Description

1. Have music playing when students arrive for class; instruct them to start moving in general space and then find a partner when the music stops playing.
2. Instruct the student pairs to find a yoga mat; one partner stands on the yoga mat, and the other stands off of the mat.
3. The partner on the mat runs to the middle area and selects a yoga pose card, then takes it back to the mat and performs that pose. Meanwhile, the other partner runs outside of the big rectangle of yoga mats (takes one lap).
4. The running student returns to the mat after doing one lap and gives his or her partner a high five. The students then switch roles—the partner who ran the lap now does the yoga pose, and the one who did the pose now runs a lap. The partners keep alternating yoga poses with running until the warm-up portion of the class is finished.

Have your students model the yoga poses!

WALL OF FLEXIBILITY

Equipment

- Photos of students performing selected stretches
- Colored construction paper
- Music

Preparation

1. Before starting the activity, select the stretching activities you want students to perform. Have students practice the stretches a few classes in advance, being sure to give them the needed cues.
2. Take pictures of students performing each stretch. Print the pictures and attach the pictures to colored paper. With each picture, include the cues for performing the stretch correctly.
3. Put three stretches on a colored piece of paper to create a poster and determine how many posters are needed for each of your classes based on the number of students in each. Put up the posters around the gym before class starts.

Description

1. Begin class by standing beside one of the posters and describing the activity to your students. Explain that they will do the stretches shown on the poster while music plays, then move to the next poster when the music stops.
2. Emphasize the importance of holding each stretch for at least 30 seconds.
3. Have the students each choose a poster to start with (ideally, no more than four students per poster) and begin performing the stretches at that poster while the music plays.
4. When the music stops, each group of students moves clockwise to the next poster.
5. The students keep moving from poster to poster for a total time of 5 to 10 minutes.

FLEXIBILITY ON THE SPOT!

Equipment

- Photos of students performing selected stretches (photos used in the previous activity may be used here)
- Large index cards
- Poly spots or computer mouse pads on which to place the stretching cards
- Pedometers (alternative provided in next section if you do not have pedometers available)

Preparation

1. Before starting this activity, select the stretching activities that you want students to perform. Have students practice the stretches a few classes in advance and be sure to give them the needed cues for correctly performing each stretch.

2. Take pictures of students performing each stretch. Print the pictures and attach them to large index cards; include on each card the cues for correctly performing that stretch.

3. Attach the index cards to poly spots or mouse pads and spread them throughout the gym.

Description

1. Instruct students that they have about 5 minutes to do as many stretches as they can. At the same time, remind them to hold each stretch for about 30 seconds and to do each stretch correctly. (Save time at the end of each class to have the present class spread out the spots for the next class!)

2. Have students wear pedometers during this activity and challenge them to accomplish a step count goal or beat the highest step count from the previous class. If you do not have pedometers available, you can challenge your students to perform as many stretches (using correct form) as they can, then challenge students in your following classes to beat the largest number of stretches accomplished in the previous class.

Body Composition and Nutrition Warm-Ups

With childhood obesity on the rise, it is crucial that physical education teachers address good nutrition as a regular part of our lesson planning. The activities presented in this section address body composition and offer great ways for students to learn about the importance of eating a well-balanced diet.

TRAVELING THROUGH THE DIGESTIVE SYSTEM

Equipment

- Hula hoops (one for each group and another to hold beanbags or cards for the entire class)
- Hula hoop holders (two per group)
- One blanket or towel per group
- Vegetable- or fruit-shaped beanbags or pictures of vegetables or fruits (one per group)
- One index card per group listing questions about digestion

Preparation

1. Divide your class into groups of no more than four members each (for extremely large classes, decide how many groups you can accommodate with the equipment available to you).

2. Prepare one index card per group that lists the following digestive activity questions:
    - What does each piece of equipment represent in the digestive system?
    - What is the function of each part of the digestive system?
    - How will one group member take a vegetable beanbag and travel through the digestive system that the group has built?

3. Teach your students the basics of the digestive system prior to doing this activity.

4. Set up a hula hoop with the question cards and all of the equipment for each group.

Description

1. Inform your students that they will use the provided equipment to build a digestive system.

2. Emphasize to each group of students that after building a digestive system they must describe what each piece of equipment represents and answer the questions

listed on the laminated cards. Stress to each group the importance of working together and listening to everyone's ideas.

3. Give the groups a time limit for building their digestive system and remind each group that someone in the group will demonstrate going through the digestive system.

4. Have a member of each group demonstrate its digestive system and describe the functions of each part as he or she travels through it.

An example of a completed digestive system.

Ideas That Work!

A Help your students learn by doing hands-on activities rather than always using paper and pencil! Building a digestive system (instead of taking a paper-and-pencil quiz) will help your students remember the part of the system and how the system functions.

CLIP-ON COMPOSITION

Equipment

- Clothespins painted blue, red, green, and yellow (one of each color for each group of students)
- Hula hoops (one for each group and another to hold clothespins in the middle of the activity area)
- Laminated signs (one for each group) listing what each colored clothespin represents and providing the following information:
  - Red (blood) takes oxygen and nutrients throughout the body. Exercise: Rev up your body and jog around the gym two times.
  - Blue (bones) exercises help your bones stay strong! Exercise: Do the Wall Sit and sing the ABC song!
  - Green (muscle) helps you move! Exercise: Pick up the jump rope with your group members (i.e., each member holds onto the rope) and jog together around the activity area two times.
  - Yellow (fat) helps your body in three ways: insulation, cushion, and fuel! Exercise: Pick up your group's paper grocery bag and go around the gym to collect six healthy food choices that contain good sources of fat.
- Paper grocery bags (one per group)
- Index cards with pictures of foods containing bad fat (e.g., hamburgers, French fries, hot dogs) and cards with pictures of foods containing good fat (e.g., salmon, peanut butter, avocados, olive oil)—enough copies of each type of card (good fat and bad fat) for each group to collect six cards total

Preparation

1. Make the signs described in the Equipment section.
2. Make index cards showing food items that represent good fat and bad fat (enough cards for each group to collect six of the good fat cards).
3. In the middle of the activity area, set up a hula hoop that contains the colored clothespins. Around the edge of the activity area, place one hula hoop for each group containing the paper grocery bag, a sign, and a jump rope.

Description

1. Spread out the colored clothespins in the hula hoop located in the center of the activity area.
2. Hold up each colored clothespin and describe what it represents (e.g., red represents blood).
3. Ask questions about the importance of having a healthy body, including the fact that being healthy involves eating some healthy fat.
4. Explain the procedure for the activity, in which each group member takes a turn coming to the hula hoop in the middle of the activity area, picking up one colored clothespin, and bringing it back to the group.

5. When the student who picked the colored clothespin comes back to the group, he or she reads the exercise that the group needs to perform together and clips the colored clothespin onto the group's paper grocery bag. The group then performs the appropriate exercise listed on the laminated Clip-On Composition sign as a group.

6. After the group finishes the exercise, the next group member goes to the hoop in the middle of the activity area to retrieve the next colored clothespin, and the group repeats step 5.

7. The group members have finished when they have clipped a clothespin of each color to their paper grocery bag and performed each of the associated exercises.

Ideas That Work!

H You can integrate recycling into your physical education classes! Use paper bags in this activity and inform your students that this is one way to use a paper bag again instead of just throwing it away. Ask the students for other ideas about how to include recycling in physical education.

CIRCLE NUTRITION

Equipment

- Paper grocery bags (one per group member)
- Hula hoops (one per group)
- Paper plates (one per group)
- One copy of the MyPlate figure for each group
- Pictures of food from each section of the MyPlate nutritional guidelines (one set of food from each section for each student group)
- Pictures of unhealthy foods (e.g., hamburgers, French fries, milkshakes, soda pop)

Preparation

1. Place the food pictures throughout your activity area (ideally, about the size of a regulation basketball court).

2. Place hula hoops (one for each group) equally distant from the center of the playing area to serve as a meeting spot for each group and a collection place for the food pictures.

3. Inside of each group's hoop, place one large paper plate and a picture of MyPlate. Beside each hoop, place a pile of paper grocery bags (enough for each student to have his or her own bag).

Description

1. Before class begins, divide your students into equal-sized groups. In class, have each group stand by a hula hoop.

2. Describe the goal of this activity: Each group fills up its paper plate with two food examples from each section of the MyPlate nutritional guidelines.

3. Each group decides which of its members will look for examples of which food group.

4. On your signal, the groups begin looking for their food examples.

5. When a group member finds the two appropriate food examples, he or she puts them into the grocery bag, runs back to the group's hula hoop, and puts the food examples on the group's paper plate.

6. Walk around to each group and ask its members to describe the food examples they found and which food groups they represent.

7. When you have checked with all of the groups, have the students spread the food examples out again in the center of the playing area for the next class.

Five Components of Fitness: Assessment

To assess students' knowledge of the five components of fitness, I use two different forms. The first one is a short four-question assessment that can be used at the end of each week (see figure 4.2). This assessment asks questions about the specific component of fitness covered during each class's warm-up time. It helps me gauge each student's level of understanding of the component in question. It also provides a place for students to think about how they can apply what they have learned during the week to their own exercise plans.

The second fitness component assessment that I use is the Fitness Friday Exercise Card (see figure 4.3 on page 76). I use this card during the Fitness Friday activity (covered in chapter 2 and earlier in this chapter). After students

---

FIGURE 4.2

Five Components of Fitness: Assessment

Name _____

1. Name the component of fitness that was covered this week in physical education class.

_____

2. Describe why it is important to include this component of fitness in your workouts.

3. How would you rate your current fitness level?

   ■ 1 point – lowest score

   ■ 5 points – highest score

   Circle your current point level: 1   2   3   4   5

4. Name an activity that you can do outside of school to improve this component of your fitness and raise your personal rating of your fitness level.

_____

From C. Gorwitz, 2012, *Teaching healthy lifestyles in middle school PE: Strategies from an award-winning program* (Champaign, IL: Human Kinetics).

FIGURE 4.3

Fitness Friday Exercise Card

Name _____

Class and teacher _____

FLEXIBILITY (6 POINTS TOTAL) _____

Pedometer steps taken _____

Exercise name _____ Completed? _____

Exercise name _____ Completed? _____

Exercise name _____ Completed? _____

Definition of flexibility (4 points total) _____

MUSCULAR STRENGTH (6 TOTAL POINTS) _____

Pedometer steps taken _____

Exercise name _____ Completed? _____

Exercise name _____ Completed? _____

Exercise name _____ Completed? _____

Definition of muscular strength (4 points total) _____

NUTRITION (6 POINTS TOTAL) _____

Pedometer steps taken _____

Exercise name _____ Completed? _____

Exercise name _____ Completed? _____

Exercise name _____ Completed? _____

Name two fruits, two vegetables, and a good source of fat (4 points) _____

EXERCISE OUTSIDE OF SCHOOL (6 TOTAL POINTS) _____

Pedometer steps taken _____

Name the exercises you did this past week for a total of 90 minutes (6 points)

_____

Name a great place in our town that you can go to exercise (4 points)

_____

Total points for the quarter _____

From C. Gorwitz, 2012, *Teaching healthy lifestyles in middle school PE: Strategies from an award-winning program* (Champaign, IL: Human Kinetics).

do their timed heart rate monitor workout, they get their Fitness Friday card and start doing the activity listed on the card. After each Fitness Friday workout, they perform a different exercise, then fill out the Fitness Friday exercise card and turn it in.

Summary

When you use the five components of fitness as the main focus of each lesson's warm-up time, you enhance your teaching in many ways. You increase the percentage of class time that your students spend in moderate to vigorous activity and promote a healthy lifestyle! Class time is precious, and none of it can be wasted. Dedicating time at the beginning of each class for a fitness component warm-up engages your students in movement with a purpose. As physical educators, we often grapple with the question of how we can deliver healthy lifestyle information without losing movement time for our students. You can resolve this dilemma by using fitness component warm-ups that teach healthy lifestyle information even as they lead more time spent in moderate and vigorous activity!

Challenge Questions

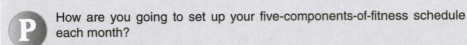 **P** How are you going to set up your five-components-of-fitness schedule each month?

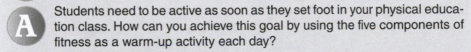 **A** Students need to be active as soon as they set foot in your physical education class. How can you achieve this goal by using the five components of fitness as a warm-up activity each day?

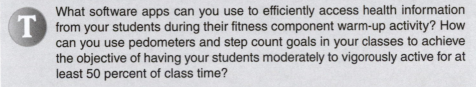 **T** What software apps can you use to efficiently access health information from your students during their fitness component warm-up activity? How can you use pedometers and step count goals in your classes to achieve the objective of having your students moderately to vigorously active for at least 50 percent of class time?

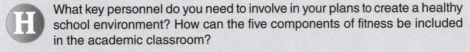 **H** What key personnel do you need to involve in your plans to create a healthy school environment? How can the five components of fitness be included in the academic classroom?

Using Heart Rate Monitors and Pedometers

Simple, inexpensive technologies can provide images of a healthy lifestyle!

This chapter provides you with time-saving tips and techniques gained from my years of experience in working with heart rate monitors and pedometers in physical education classes. I share with you here my best organizational tips for integrating these technologies into your classes as efficiently as possible. The chapter also presents step-by-step lesson plans that you can easily use in your classes right now!

Authentic assessment is an essential tool to use in physical education classes, and heart rate monitors and pedometers give you the data you need not only to assess students but also to provide them with valuable information about their health. This chapter covers rubric templates that include authentic assessment of students' fitness levels, and you can use these rubrics with any unit you teach. The chapter also addresses pedometer step count goals and efficient strategies for recording key information.

Approach the PATH . . .

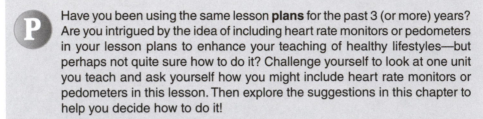

P Have you been using the same lesson **plans** for the past 3 (or more) years? Are you intrigued by the idea of including heart rate monitors or pedometers in your lesson plans to enhance your teaching of healthy lifestyles—but perhaps not quite sure how to do it? Challenge yourself to look at one unit you teach and ask yourself how you might include heart rate monitors or pedometers in this lesson. Then explore the suggestions in this chapter to help you decide how to do it!

A Are your students moderately or vigorously **active** for at least 50 percent of their class time? Are you looking for ways to motivate your students to move? Challenge yourself to write down one idea for using pedometers or heart rate monitors in one of your lessons. Then, while reading this chapter, look for the ways you can accomplish your goal of increasing students' movement in your physical education classes.

T Are you afraid of or just shy about using **technology** in your classes? Or, perhaps, have you used technology but found that it took too much time out of your teaching? Challenge yourself to write down one area in which you can include technology in your lesson planning (e.g., organization, implementation, lesson ideas). Then use the ideas in this chapter to help you accomplish this goal.

H In your school district, many people are using technology effectively, and they do not have to be in the physical education department. Challenge yourself to write down one person you can talk to about using technology in your classes, or someone who can give you ideas about funding the purchase of heart rate monitors to get your program started! As you read this chapter, write down questions to ask the person you named.

Heart Rate Monitors

As discussed in chapter 2, heart rate monitors can be a wonderful tool in physical education. For one thing, they give students instant information about their heart rates as they exercise. Of course, students will not always have a heart rate monitor to use outside of school, but the key is using it as a tool in physical education class to learn how their bodies feel when they exercise properly! Heart rate monitors also give you invaluable information about your students' fitness levels—you can walk around your class and look at each student's heart rate monitor to see how he or she is doing. Heart rate monitors also help all students to be successful in physical education class, regardless of whether they are out of shape or athletically gifted. Everyone in class can work out in his or her target heart rate zone. Some students will need to run more, whereas others can stay in their zone simply by jogging!

You can use data from a student's heart rate monitor in many valuable ways. During class, the monitor provides instant information about the student's heart rate and whether he or she is meeting the goal of exercising moderately or vigorously for fifty percent of class time. You can have your students wear the monitors for the entire class in order to obtain information. You can also use heart rate data after class to learn more about how to structure your lessons to increase your students' time spent exercising.

I have been using heart rate monitors in my physical education program for a long time. I started out small and worked hard to fund my current program. Don't be intimidated by the potential cost—by starting small, you can make it happen! When I began using heart rate monitors, I found out about a conference in Fargo, North Dakota, that included with registration a Polar heart rate monitor. If you brought five people from your school, you got a sixth heart rate monitor for free. Two other physical education teachers from my school and I recruited two more teachers and drove to Fargo for the conference. Yes, you have to be a dedicated teacher (or crazy!) to spend 10 hours riding in a car, but the people with whom I teach are phenomenal. We always have fun together, so it was a great adventure. The conference was awesome, and we met a lot of other physical education teachers and learned a lot. My school district paid for the conference, and I started my program with those six heart rate monitors!

I began by dividing my classes into four groups (six members per group) and assigning each group a color. When the students arrived for class, I had posted a colored piece of construction paper on the wall to let them know which group would wear the heart rate monitors that day. Nowadays, I have my students wear the heart rate monitors once a week during our Fitness Friday activities. I have also used them in various lesson ideas that have worked extremely well.

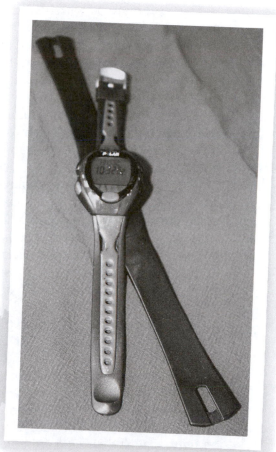

This is the type of heart rate monitor I use in my classes. It can record the amount of time the student has spent working in the specified target heart rate zone, as well as time spent above and below, and the average heart rate.

You can look for grants to provide funds for starting your program. My state's physical education association (Wisconsin Health and Physical Education) offers small grants for purchasing equipment such as heart rate monitors. I have won several of these grants to purchase equipment to improve my program. Contact your state association to see if it offers grants to purchase equipment. Another source of funding might be found in your community. Local businesses are often looking to help out the schools in their communities. You could ask your local chamber of commerce for names of local businesses that might be willing to help you to start your heart rate monitor program. You can use the latest obesity statistics as a strong reason for purchasing the monitors. Businesses are looking to fund programs that will really make a difference, and heart rate monitors fit the bill.

Using equipment in classrooms can present a management challenge, and that's certainly true of heart rate monitors. I don't want my students to waste time in trying to find and attach their monitor—that's time they could be engaged in activity! So I've made it a priority to work out a management system that makes it easy for the students and for me to track and use the monitors. Specifically, I have a cart that a fellow teacher (Marcia Schmidt) designed that holds the heart rate monitors. Attached to the front of the cart is a piece of plywood with hooks that hold the heart rate monitors (the hooks are labeled with numbers and the corresponding heart rate monitor hangs there). The elastic straps needed for wearing the monitors are kept in a large bucket next to the cart. The students are each assigned a number for their monitor (and their pedometer) based on the numbered roster provided by our computerized grading system. I assign the numbers and show students where the monitors are located on the first day of class. To use the monitors, students come out of the locker room, get their numbered heart rate monitor and a properly sized elastic strap, return to the locker room to put them on, and then come back out of the locker room ready to start.

When beginning your program, allow time in your lesson plans for your students to practice using the heart rate monitors and for talking with them about how they will use the monitors in class. Depending on your students' ages, they may also need time at the beginning of each year to practice putting on the monitors and working out in their target heart rate zones. I have found it best to teach students step by step how to put on the heart rate monitor, and I spend the first part of each day in the beginning reviewing this material (regardless of grade level). The following description covers a fitting lesson for the transmitter (chest strap); this process takes most of one class period.

First, I have the students get only the transmitter (chest strap) and the stretch band that attaches to it and sit down in front of me (no monitor at this time!). Next, I have them lay the stretch band on the floor in front of them so that they can hold only the transmitter. I inform them that the transmitter sends their heart rate information to their monitor. Then I have them look at the transmitter's back side, which is ridged. I explain that the ridges must be tight against their skin (with younger students, describe what you mean by tight). This is the hardest part for the students to understand—and also the biggest source of problems when working with the heart monitors. I then hold the transmitter up to my body and show the students where it should be located (next to the heart, of course!). Then I have the students hold their transmitters against their bodies (outside of their clothes) so that I can make sure they are in the correct position.

(A) Give students time to become familiar with the parts of the heart rate monitor and how they are used. (B) Have students demonstrate that they know the correct positioning for the monitor. (C) Students should practice attaching the stretch band several times.

Now you are ready to teach your students how to put the stretch band through the hole on the side of the transmitter. The students should hold the transmitter in their hands and work on this. I have them practice attaching the stretch band several times while I walk around and answer questions. I have also found it best to identify several students who are good at putting on the stretch band and have them go around the class to help others (this approach empowers these students to be leaders in the class).

Next, I have the students lay their transmitters and stretch bands on the floor in front of them and watch me put my monitor on my body (on the outside of my shirt). I tell them that the first step is to put a bit of water on the heart monitor (for conduction), then I put the monitor on myself so that they can see for themselves what it should look like. I then ask for students (both boys and girls) who know how to put on the transmitter correctly and I watch them put their monitors on over their clothes. If they do it correctly, they are the designated helpers who can work with other students who are struggling (of course, the helpers do not touch the other students but just give them verbal instructions!).

The students then go to the locker rooms and put on their transmitters (if you have no locker rooms available, find separate private areas where the boys and the girls can put on their transmitters). When the students return from the locker rooms (or private areas), they put on their monitors (the watch part) and show me that they have a heart rate at the bottom of their watch. I then have them do a 5-minute workout (just jogging and walking), during which I walk around the gym (or other designated area) and ask the students to stop and show me their monitor to make sure it is working. I have the helpers start a couple of minutes later so that they can help me answer questions in the beginning (thus the helpers end up doing a 3-minute workout).

At the end of class, I show everyone how to clean the monitors. I have two buckets (on top of a cart)—one with soapy water, the other with clear water. Attached to the side of the cart are two towels. I demonstrate dunking the transmitter (only the transmitter) into the soapy water and swishing it around, then dunking it into the clean water and swishing it around again, before drying it off with a towel and putting it back in its place on the heart rate monitor cart. The students then take turns cleaning their transmitters and drying them off. If any class time remains, I have the students do a cardiorespiratory endurance activity.

The following examples of heart rate monitor lessons have worked really well in my middle school classes. They can be modified to work at the high school level as well.

Ideas That Work!

P You can use heart rate monitors as an authentic assessment tool! The great thing about the monitors is that they are not subjective—the time that a student has spent in his or her target heart rate zone is shown right there on the monitor. Students are all graded based on the same criteria, and no one can say that you graded them differently. See chapter 2 for more details about how you can use heart rate monitors for assessment!

12-MINUTE FITNESS RUN/WALK

Equipment

- Cones
- Heart rate monitors
- Pedometers

Preparation

1. Use cones to set up a run/walk course in a large space (indoor or outdoor). The specific course layout depends on the area in which you are teaching. If you are teaching outside, the course should be on a flat surface and form the shape of a square (not too big because you need to be able to see the students and talk with them). If you are teaching in a gymnasium, the course should be the size of a regulation basketball court. I suggest that you put on a monitor and walk fast to see how many laps you do in 12 minutes.

2. Before class starts, make a list of pairs for your students to work in. One student in each pair wears a heart rate monitor; the other wears a pedometer. If you have an odd number of students, you can either act as the coach and motivator for one student or arrange one group of three, in which two students wear a heart rate monitor.

Description

1. Give the students wearing a heart rate monitor some time to get their heart rate up into their target heart rate zone. Meanwhile, have the students wearing pedometers do some stretching and show you that their pedometer reading is zero.

2. When the students wearing a monitor have their heart rates in their target heart rate zone, start the stopwatch and have the students wearing pedometers join in the activity. The students wearing a monitor run clockwise outside the cones. The students wearing a pedometer run counterclockwise inside the cones. Everyone works out for 12 minutes. (You can vary the time depending on the length of your class period.)

3. The students wearing pedometers act as coaches and motivators for their partners wearing heart rate monitors. The coaches cheer on their partners and encourage them every step of the way. They can ask their partners what their heart rates are and how they are feeling. If a partner's heart rate is on the low end of the target heart rate zone, the coach can give him or her tips for moving faster; on the other hand, if the heart rate is too high, the coach can help the partner by telling him or her to slow down a little. It is amazing how much cheering students do during this activity! It is really fun to see how concerned the students are about their partners and what tools they use to motivate them!

4. On the second day, have the partners switch roles and repeat the activity.

5. Base the students' grades on how long they stay in their target heart rate zone. You can also set a step count goal for them to achieve during this activity and grade them based on their pedometer step count. I have set step count goals by walking the course as fast as I can for 12 minutes and using my step count as the step count goal for the class.

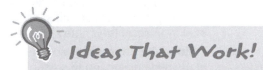

Ideas That Work!

P Have students do a workout that emphasizes a concept you are working on in class (e.g., the FIT principle).

TWO-BY-TWO FIT

Equipment

- Two-by-Two FIT worksheets (one for every two students; see figure 5.1)
- Heart rate monitors (one per student or pair of students)
- Pedometers (one per student or pair of students)
- Big exercise balls (one for each student in a group)
- Jump ropes (one for each student in a group)
- Exercise bikes (if available, for the cardiorespiratory endurance activity; one for each student in a group)
- Medicine balls (or alternatives, such as hand weights; one for each student in a group)
- Stretchy exercise bands (one for each student in a group)
- Descriptions of 6 big-ball flexibility activities to post on the wall for the exercise ball station

Preparation

1. Make copies of the Two-by-Two Fit worksheet (see figure 5.1).
2. Set up all the Two-by-Two stations. Remember that the goal of each physical education class is to have no one standing around; with this in mind, the number of stations depends on the number of students you have! For example, if you have 24 students, 4 stations would be an appropriate number; if you have 48 students, 8 stations would be needed. Here are examples of stations that I use for this activity (the sample worksheet in figure 5.1 matches these stations):

   • **Flexibility.** Place one big exercise ball per group member at the station. Place posters showing ball exercises—one poster per group member—on the wall at the station. The students read the description of each exercise, then perform the activities without trying to work a specific target heart rate zone. The heart monitor is used simply as a way for each student to see what his or her heart rate is while performing each activity.

   • **Cardiorespiratory endurance.** Each student gets on an exercise bike and starts pedaling. When their heart rate reaches their target heart rate, they start their heart rate monitor. The students keep their heart rates in their designated target heart rate zone (for example, in my middle school classes, the target zone is 150 to 190). The students exercise for 3 minutes, then stop. Each student records his or her time spent in the target heart rate zone on the worksheet.

   • **Cardiorespiratory endurance.** Place one jump rope per group member at the station. Students jump until their heart rate reaches their target heart rate zone, then start their monitor and jump for 3 minutes. When they have finished jumping, students record their time spent in the target heart rate zone.

   • **Muscular strength.** Place medicine balls and resistance bands (one per pair) at the station. Reminded students that they are not to work out in a specific target heart rate zone but simply to start their heart rate monitor and then record their heart rate at the end of their 6-minute workout. Students time their medicine ball exercise for 3 minutes, then pick up the stretchy band and exercise for 3 minutes. When the students stop their heart rate monitor, the time will read 6 minutes. Students record their results.

FIGURE 5.1

Two-by-Two FIT Worksheet

Name_____ Partner _____

Your teacher will assign you a partner. You and your partner will each put on your heart rate monitors and pedometers. You will be working on the FIT principle today. Remember that this acronym stands for frequency, intensity, and time. You will be doing several activities and recording your heart rate after you have done each one. Thus you will learn how different activities affect your heart rate! You will also learn that the intensity of your workout affects your heart rate.

PEDOMETER

You will also wear a pedometer today and record the number of steps you take. You are not graded on your steps. Try to take as many steps as you can!

ACTIVITIES

1. **Flexibility.** Look at the exercise posters on the wall. Choose one of the big ball exercises to do, but do not try to work out in your target heart rate zone. You will simply use your heart monitor as a tool to see what your heart rate is when you use the exercise ball. Start your heart rate monitor and spend 3 minutes at this station.

    Record your heart rate at the end of 3 minutes _____

2. **Cardiorespiratory endurance.** You and your partner each get on an exercise bike and start pedaling. When your heart rate reaches your target heart rate zone, start your monitor. Exercise for 3 more minutes, then push the blue button to stop. Both of you now take your papers to your teacher and show him or her your monitor. Your teacher will record your time in your target heart rate zone.

    Time in your target heart rate zone _____

3. **Cardiorespiratory endurance.** You and your partner each get a jump rope and start jumping. When your heart rate reaches your target heart rate zone, start your monitor. Jump rope for 3 more minutes, then push the blue button to stop. Go to your teacher, and he or she will record the time you spent in your target heart rate zone.

    Time in your target heart rate zone _____

4. **Muscular strength.** You and your partner get one medicine ball. Start your heart rate monitor and exercise with the medicine ball and the stretchy bands for 3 minutes, then push the blue button to stop.

    Record your heart rate at the end of 3 minutes _____

    Total time in your target heart rate zone _____ Grade _____

    Total pedometer steps (record) _____

From C. Gorwitz, 2012, *Teaching healthy lifestyles in middle school PE: Strategies from an award-winning program* (Champaign, IL: Human Kinetics).

Description

The title of this activity really explains what it is all about! Two students work together, each wearing a heart rate monitor and pedometer. (If you do not have enough heart rate monitors or pedometers, this lesson can be done over two class periods, thus allowing the partners to switch roles after the first day). The lesson also focuses on the FIT principle (frequency, intensity, and time). As the partners move to different stations, they use the monitor and pedometer to gather information while performing the exercises. Thus the students learn what their heart rate is while performing different exercises, as well as how the intensity level of their exercise can affect their heart rate.

HEART-SMART ORIENTEERING

You can use this activity during any unit that you teach; this example addresses a pickleball unit. This unit demonstrates how you can incorporate heart rate monitors into any lesson along with skill practice. You could also incorporate the skill of orienteering into this activity by having the students use a compass to locate all of the cardinal directions.

Equipment

- Index cards (one per group)
- Heart-Smart Orienteering worksheets (one per student; see figure 5.2 on page 90)
- Heart-Smart Orienteering instruction sheets (one per station)
- Colored paper
- Pens or pencils (one per group)
- Heart rate monitors and pedometers (one per student or, if necessary, shared)
- Hand weights, big exercise balls, medicine balls
- Exercise bikes (or other cardio equipment), jump ropes, aerobic steppers
- Equipment needed for the skill being taught (e.g., balls, nets, and rackets for pickleball)

Preparation

1. Prepare an index card for each group listing colors (one color for each station). Each group's card must list the colors in a different order from the other groups' cards so that each group starts at a different point. To make the index cards, I simply use a marker to put a small amount of each color on the card. For example, group 1's card could look like this: orange, green, purple, yellow, black, blue, and red. Group 2's card could look like this: green,

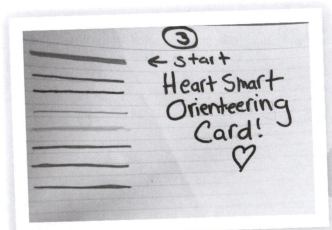

← start
Heart Smart
Orienteering
Card!
♡

Each group's index card should list the colors in a different order.

purple, yellow, black, blue, red, and orange. Proceed in this manner to make one index card for each group of students.

2. Make copies of the Heart-Smart Orienteering worksheet (figure 5.2 on page 90).

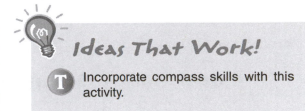

Ideas That Work!

T Incorporate compass skills with this activity.

3. Set up each station. Tape the colored Heart-Smart Orienteering instruction sheet indicating the compass direction and instructions to the correct wall (e.g., tape the north sheet to the north wall in the activity area). Place the equipment for each station beside each colored direction sheet.

Description

1. Before doing the activity, have students put on their heart rate monitors and pedometers. Divide the students into groups (ideally, four to six students so everyone is participating at the same time). Give each group an index card and each student an orienteering sheet.

2. Tell the students that they will go to colored stations in the order indicated on their card. Go over the Heart-Smart Orienteering worksheet (see figure 5.2 on page 90), explaining that at each station they are to answer the question posed on the sheet and do the skill at the station. They will turn in their sheets at the end of class.

3. Each group starts by locating the colored heart-smart instruction sheet for the first color shown on its index card. For example, if the first color shown on the card is orange, then the group looks around the room and locates the orange sheet taped to the wall, then jogs as a group to that sheet. The group then reads the instructions on the sheet and performs the indicated activity. When everyone in the group has done the activity, they record their heart rate and pedometer step count using their own heart rate monitor and pedometer. This is a self-paced activity. When the whole group has done the listed skill, they each record their own heart rate and pedometer step count, then move as a group to the next colored station listed on their index card.

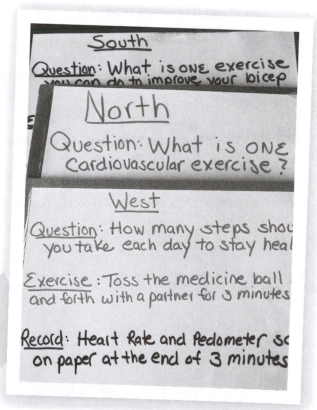

South
Question: What is one exercise
you can do to improve your bicep

North
Question: What is one
Cardiovascular exercise?

West
Question: How many steps shou
you take each day to stay heal

Exercise: Toss the medicine ball
and forth with a partner for 3 minutes

Record: Heart Rate and Pedometer sc
on paper at the end of 3 minutes

Instruction sheets include the compass direction, a question to answer, an exercise to perform, and instructions for recording heart rate and pedometer step count.

FIGURE 5.2

Heart-Smart Orienteering Worksheet

Name _____

Starting heart rate _____ Finishing heart rate _____

1. North (blue)

Question: When making a forehand shot in pickleball, should your arm be straight or bent?

Answer: _____

Pickleball skill practice: Practice the forehand shot against the wall with a partner.

Heart rate _____ Pedometer step count _____

2. South (red)

Question: Name one exercise you can do to improve your biceps strength for pickleball.

Answer: _____

Pickleball skill practice: Use the racket to practice the following skills: (1) bouncing the ball in the air with your palm up and (2) bouncing the ball on the floor with your palm down.

Heart rate _____ Pedometer step count _____

3. East (orange)

Question: What is the target heart rate zone we are using in physical education class?

Answer: _____

Cardiorespiratory endurance exercise: Jog for 3 minutes inside the cones on the basketball court.

Heart rate _____ Pedometer step count _____

From C. Gorwitz, 2012, *Teaching healthy lifestyles in middle school PE: Strategies from an award-winning program* (Champaign, IL: Human Kinetics).

4. West (green)

Question: The backhand shot in pickleball is used when you hit the ball on the side of your body that the racket is on. True or false?

Answer: _____

Pickleball skill practice: Practice the backhand shot over the net with a partner.

Heart rate _____ Pedometer step count _____

5. Northeast (purple)

Question: How many total steps should you take each day to stay healthy?

Answer: _____

Cardiorespiratory endurance exercise: Jump rope forward for 2 minutes.

Heart rate _____ Pedometer step count_____

6. Southwest (yellow)

Question: What is one cardiorespiratory endurance exercise you do outside of school?

Answer: _____

Cardiorespiratory endurance exercise: Jump rope backward for 2 minutes.

Heart rate _____ Pedometer step count _____

7. Southeast (black)

Question: What are the five components of fitness?

Answer: _____

Cardiorespiratory endurance exercise: Run and touch 5 lines in the gym.

Heart rate _____ Pedometer steps _____

From C. Gorwitz, 2012, *Teaching healthy lifestyles in middle school PE: Strategies from an award-winning program* (Champaign, IL: Human Kinetics).

FITNESS SOCCER

Have your students wear their heart rate monitors while playing 4v4 soccer and have them remain in their target heart rate zone for a specified time (depending on the length of your class period). This activity gives students information about how they should play the game to improve their cardiorespiratory endurance. Before doing this activity, you would give lessons teaching basic soccer skills and provide students with time to practice using those skills. You would also have students play soccer lead-up games that prepare them to play small-sided (4v4) soccer games.

Equipment

- Heart rate monitors
- Pedometers
- Soccer balls
- Cones to mark the boundary lines of each soccer field

Preparation

Set up several small soccer fields next to each other with cones marking the boundary lines. It is best to have as many small fields as possible so that all students can participate at the same time, and the dimensions of the fields do not matter (they should not be regulation soccer fields).

Description

1. When your students arrive for class, have them put on their heart rate monitors and pedometers. When all students have their pedometer set to zero and a heart rate displayed on their monitor, you are ready to start class.
2. Announce the pedometer step count goal for the day.
3. Tell students the designated target heart rate zone for playing the small-sided soccer games today. Announce the length of the small-sided games and instruct students to keep their heart rate in the target heart rate zone for the entire game.
4. Each small field will have two teams of four students each (one student will play the goalie position).
5. Have the students warm up by jogging, then start your stopwatch to time the workout.
6. At the end of the designated time, blow your whistle to signal the students to stop their heart rate monitors. Next, have the students keep playing (but not restarting their heart rate monitors) while you go to one field at a time and record the students' time spent in the target heart rate zone.
7. Students continue to wear their heart rate monitors and play the small-sided soccer games until the end of class, when they take off the monitors and clean them.

Pedometers

Like heart rate monitors, pedometers have become vital tools in my PE classes. They offer a simple, effective way to help students learn to be aware of their level of activity. And they're an excellent authentic assessment tool.

Numbering the pedometers helps in managing their use.

My students wear their pedometers every day in class. On the first day of class, I assign each of my students a number for their pedometer (the same number as their heart rate monitor). The pedometers are kept in separate numbered sections of a plastic box. The student can easily see which pedometer is theirs by finding their number in the box. They know that as soon as they come out of the locker room they are to put on their pedometer. The correct way to put on a pedometer is to slide it onto your shorts or pants at the waist. To work correctly, the pedometer must be level, which means that it cannot be placed sideways on a pocket. The pedometer also needs to be placed in the middle of the leg, not on the side of the waist.

I give each class a step goal to achieve that day. After averaging the steps over many class periods, the minimum number of steps I use for a goal is 1,500. You should use information from your students' pedometers to determine the minimum number of steps to use as a goal in your own physical education classes. I have recorded the step count goals for all my students. Doing this doesn't take very long, and it gives me an invaluable tool for learning which students are really moving during class and which are just standing around.

I have found that the best way to grade my students on pedometers is to include the step count as part of my rubrics. In the past, I have recorded step counts for my students every day, but that approach took too much time, and I wasn't using the recorded steps for anything. Now, I record the pedometer step counts at least three times during each unit that I teach, and the students do not know which day's count I am recording until the end of that class period. I have my students show me their pedometers, and we discuss their daily step counts, but I do not record them every day.

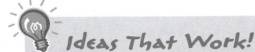

Ideas That Work!

A Use pedometers to do roll call! I do not need my students to sit in squads or roll call lines in order to take attendance. Instead, because each student is assigned a numbered pedometer, I can look in my pedometer box, see which pedometers are left, and know that those students are absent.

Ideas That Work!

P Record pedometer step counts in an organized and accurate manner! I have tried many ways of recording pedometer step counts. Here is the best idea that I have ever used: I now have my students line up at the end of class in alphabetic order (that is also how I number my pedometers), take off their pedometers, and put them on the ground at their feet. The pedometer case should be open so that the number of steps is showing. Anyone who is shaking the pedometer receives a zero (once usually does the trick!). I walk down the line and record the number of steps. After I have recorded a student's step count, he or she can pick up the pedometer, set it to zero, and put it away. This procedure takes only a couple of minutes, and after the first few times the class knows which order to stand in, so it really doesn't take any time at all!

Another advantage of including pedometer step counts in my rubrics is that the students and their parents have concrete proof of movement during that unit's assessment. For example, when parents asks me how their student received a certain grade, I can show them that the student took only, say, 700 steps toward a goal of 1,500. This information shows parents that their student was just standing around instead of moving. Of course, the 700 would represent an average, because I take the step counts at least three times during each unit; as a result, a parent (or the student) cannot complain, for example, that the student was sick on the day that I assessed steps, because two other days were also included in that portion of the rubric.

Figure 5.3 shows a sample rubric and how the pedometer step counts are assessed. I have chosen a simple rubric for football so that you can see how the steps would be assessed in a game that most schools teach. The rubric addresses a small-sided (5v5) football game with a quarterback and four other players. I have a lot of games going at once so that the students can get as many steps as possible.

Another way to use pedometers as an authentic assessment tool is to have your students record their pedometer step counts for each activity they do. Doing so provides them with valuable information about how much movement

Ideas That Work!

A Use pedometers to improve your teaching! How much time do you think you spend on giving directions or stopping your class to have students listen to you? Do a little study of your own by having one class start the activity for the day as soon as possible and trying to stop them only minimally to give instruction and record the pedometer step counts at the end of the class period. In the next class, give more lengthy instructions and stop the class more often to give instruction and see what their pedometer step counts are. Then compare the two classes and see how many more steps the first class took. This experiment will help you prioritize devoting as little time as reasonably possible to instruction so that most of your class time can be spent in movement!

FIGURE 5.3

Sixth-Grade Football Rubric

Name _____

Area assessed	Advanced	Proficient	Basic	
Skill—NASPE standards 1 and 2	3 points	2 points	1 point	
Throw	Grips the ball with thumb and index finger on back and other fingers on laces, and nondominant side faces target. Steps forward with the foot opposite the throwing arm.	Grips the ball with thumb and index finger in the middle of the ball, and nondominant side faces target 80 percent of the time. Steps forward with the foot opposite the throwing arm.	Grips the ball with thumb and index finger not on the back of the ball, and nondominant side does not face target. Steps forward with same-side foot as throwing arm.	
Spiral	Ball spirals tightly through the air on release.	Ball does not spiral tightly.	Ball wobbles through the air.	
Follow-through	Arm goes across body with pinky coming off last.	Arm does not go across body with pinky coming off last.	Arm goes directly down the side of the body.	
Catch	Catches the ball 90 percent of the time or better with hands out away from the body.	Catches the ball 80 percent of the time with hands halfway out from the body.	Catches the ball less than 50 percent of the time; hands are not out away from the body.	
			TOTAL	
Strategy and good sporting behavior—NASPE standards 2 and 5	6 points	3 points	1 point	
Written work	Describes three strategies used during a football game.	Describes two strategies used during a football game.	Describes one strategy used during a football game.	
	Describes three types of good sporting behavior that the student will use during game play.	Describes two types of good sporting behavior that the student will use during game play.	Describes one type of good sporting behavior that the student will use during game play.	
			TOTAL	
Fitness— NASPE standards 3, 4, and 6	6 points	3 points	1 point	
Pedometer step count (average the pedometer scores recorded three times during the unit)	3,000 or more	2,999–2,500	2,499 or fewer	
Written work	Describes how three or more components of fitness can be achieved during game play.	Describes how two components of fitness can be achieved during game play.	Describes how one component of fitness can be achieved during game play.	
			TOTAL	
			TOTAL SCORE	

From C. Gorwitz, 2012, *Teaching healthy lifestyles in middle school PE: Strategies from an award-winning program* (Champaign, IL: Human Kinetics).

they are achieving in each unit. Rather than getting lectured by their teacher (you!), they will simply see the count of steps they took during each activity and be able to compare them (e.g., the number of steps taken during a 4v4 soccer game compared to those taken in a volleyball game)!

Figure 5.4 shows a comparison assessment activity that I use in my physical education classes. Each student's portfolio includes a copy of the assessment, which lists the units for that academic quarter. In order to access the sheets during the quarter, I paper clip them together and put them in front of that class's portfolios. I also color-coordinate each quarter's sheets (e.g., first quarter's sheets are printed on green paper, second quarter's sheets on yellow paper, third quarter's sheets on blue paper, and fourth quarter's sheets on pink paper) so I can see at a glance which is which. I record pedometer steps at least three times during each unit. On the selected recording day, I have the comparison sheets ready for students to record the number of steps they took that day. At the end of the quarter, the students fill out the analysis questions at the bottom of the assessment, and we discuss their answers. It is powerful for students to identify the activities in which they took more steps—in other words, in which activities they move more. I record the number of pedometer steps they have taken during each activity as part of my written grade.

One way in which I've consistently used pedometers to create fun activities is to invent themed walks. You can use any theme from any subject! Pick out a theme for your pedometer walk that everyone in your area of the country would get excited about. For example, for one walk I chose a March Madness theme for two reasons. First, I love watching basketball, and so do most of my students. Also, in Wisconsin in March, there is snow still on the ground, and we have cabin fever really bad! This activity gives us something exciting to look forward to in class during March when we really want to get outside but it is still too cold!

Ideas That Work!

H Talk to classroom teachers about ideas for themed walks! One example is the Heartbeat Walk. For this activity, math teachers design a lesson in which students research how many times an average heart beats per minute, use prediction skills to calculate how long it would take them to walk a mile (or 2 or 3 miles), and then calculate the total number of times their heart would beat while walking a 1-mile course. They can then calculate how many beats there would be for their entire class or for the whole school. After students do this math lesson, the entire school can participate in a 1-mile Heartbeat Walk! Another possibility, this one using a language arts theme, is the Poetry Walk. For this activity, the language arts teachers design a lesson in which students list descriptive words that can be used in writing a poem about being outside and walking. The language arts teachers then provide students with a map of a 1-mile walking course and, during the walk, have them write on the map what they observe while out on the walk, as well as words describing their feelings while walking. After the walk, the students write their poems. You could build on this idea by laminating the students' poems, placing them on the ground along the walking course, and having them do the walk a second time, during which they pause and read the poems along the way.

FIGURE 5.4

Pedometer Step Comparison
Pedometer Steps—7th Grade (First Quarter)

Name _____

Name of activity	Steps taken	What could you have done to take more steps today?
Ultimate Frisbee		
Speedball		
PACER test		
Fitness Friday		

In which activity did you take the most steps?

_____

In which activity did you take the fewest steps?

_____

What exercises do you do outside of school that would help improve your fitness level and also help you take more steps in class?

_____

MARCH MADNESS: FOLLOW THE BOUNCING BALL

Equipment

- Pedometers (one per student or pair of students)
- Bulletin board or other area in which to post college basketball teams and mileage (or map)
- Names of the men's and women's teams competing in the NCAA Division I Basketball Championship tournaments

Preparation

1. During the NCAA basketball tournaments in March, you can plan an activity using pedometer step counts to imagine a walk to a selected college participating in the tournament. Gather the names of the men's and women's teams participating in the tournament and choose one college for each class that you teach. Pick colleges that your students could walk to in the number of days you have allotted for this activity.

2. Determine how far it is from your school to each of the chosen colleges. Post each college's name and the distance to it on the bulletin board in your gym (or other designated area in your school). As an alternative, you could use the same college for all of your classes and combine the steps taken in each class to achieve the number of steps needed.

3. You could also use your teacher web page to post extra credit mileage questions about your selected college(s).

4. Plan a culminating activity for this challenge. Possibilities include basketball shooting games and trivia questions. The following description is an example of this activity, although the culminating activity can be anything you come up with! Combine totals from these activities with the number of miles walked to determine the champion.

Description

Each team is stationed at their own basket with colored poly spots on the floor for students to shoot from (e.g., one at the free-throw line, one at the three-point line, and one underneath the basket). Each basket should have the same number of poly spots positioned in the same way. Each team chooses half of its members to shoot from the poly spots and half to answer basketball trivia questions. Including basketball trivia in the activity provides an alternative for students who may not be as comfortable shooting baskets to participate and help their team. We never want a student to be embarrassed while they are participating in an activity and by giving teams a nonathletic skill option, all of the team members can participate and have fun!

Summary

By using heart rate monitors and pedometers in your physical education classes, you can provide your students with valuable information to help them lead a healthy lifestyle. In taking this approach, you are not just talking about the concept of heart rate to your students but using the monitors to show your students their own heart rates while they are exercising. The monitors also serve as great tools to provide all students—regardless of skill level or athletic ability—the chance to succeed in physical education class and to apply that information in their lives outside of class. Using the heart rate monitors helps students develop the confidence they need in order to become lifetime movers! Pedometers also provide an awesome tool that not only tells your students how many steps they take during class but also provides you with valuable information about how affective your lessons are in getting your students to be moderately or vigorously active during at least 50 percent of class time. You can also use pedometers as authentic assessment tools in grading your students on their fitness. In short, heart rate monitors and pedometers are invaluable tools that can help both you and your students lead healthier lives!

Challenge Questions

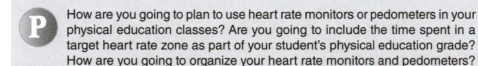

P How are you going to plan to use heart rate monitors or pedometers in your physical education classes? Are you going to include the time spent in a target heart rate zone as part of your student's physical education grade? How are you going to organize your heart rate monitors and pedometers?

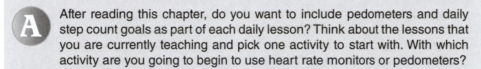

A After reading this chapter, do you want to include pedometers and daily step count goals as part of each daily lesson? Think about the lessons that you are currently teaching and pick one activity to start with. With which activity are you going to begin to use heart rate monitors or pedometers?

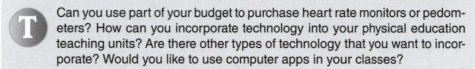

T Can you use part of your budget to purchase heart rate monitors or pedometers? How can you incorporate technology into your physical education teaching units? Are there other types of technology that you want to incorporate? Would you like to use computer apps in your classes?

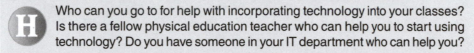

H Who can you go to for help with incorporating technology into your classes? Is there a fellow physical education teacher who can help you to start using technology? Do you have someone in your IT department who can help you?

chapter 6

Staff Wellness

Follow the PATH way
to a successful wellness program!

It's not just kids who can benefit from encouragement to live healthy lifestyles. Adults often need and want to find ways to enhance their well-being too. Take your fellow teachers, for example—many of them are very dedicated and don't usually set aside time for themselves. If you can offer programs at your school site, you will make it much easier for them to participate! You will also find that providing opportunities for your colleagues to improve their health improves staff morale! You can contribute to your colleagues' overall wellness in a variety of ways.

The first step in **planning** a staff wellness program is to conduct a staff wellness survey (I suggest doing so online since it is more convenient, meaning you are likely to get more responses) to help you analyze your colleagues' needs. The survey should be short (many staff members will not take a long survey) and should ask the following questions:

1. What activities would you like to see offered? (Provide several choices and a blank space for respondents to write in other answers.)
2. When should wellness activities take place—before school, after school, or a combination?
3. Would you be willing to lead an activity? Or do you know community members who would be willing to do so for free for or a small fee?
4. Would you be willing to serve on the school's wellness planning committee?

Once the survey is completed, contact the people who expressed interest in serving on the wellness committee and start planning your first activity!

 When I started our staff wellness program, I offered **activities** that I thought the staff would really like. Nonetheless, the turnout was very low, and I received some very good advice that I will share with you now. The activities you offer to staff members should be things that *they* are interested in, not what you (or whoever is in charge of staff wellness) may be interested in. Use ideas from the survey and start small. Start out with one activity a month and see what the turnout is. Ask the people who come to the first few activities what they think about the program and how it might be improved. Start small and move slowly!

You can use **technology** in various ways to promote staff wellness. Here are a few examples: offering wellness tips as part of the school's morning announcements; creating a staff wellness web page; setting up an online checkout system for heart rate monitors, pedometers, and other exercise equipment; using software to conduct fitness testing for staff members. If your school e-mails the morning announcements to your staff, you can include tips for fitness and healthy living every Monday! Talk to your school librarian to find out how fitness equipment can be set up with barcodes and checked out by staff members. Design a simple staff wellness web page that offers wellness tips, healthy recipes, and exercise offerings in your community. You can also offer your staff the same fitness testing you use with your students, as well as follow-up classes to address the meaning of the test results and how staff members can use them to improve their health.

 It is important to offer staff members an environment marked by **harmony** where they feel safe in learning about how to lead a healthy lifestyle. People do not want to be preached at about all the things they are doing wrong or how overweight they are! Instead, take a fun approach. One great way to start a wellness program is to organize an activity, such as a staff bowling night, where everyone is laughing and having a good time. Staff members who participate will come back to school and share about how much fun they had and how excited they are about the next activity. You can then build on that success with a before-school walk followed by a healthy snack. Starting out small and building on each successful activity is the right path to follow!

Getting Started

You may have a lot of ideas for your staff wellness program, but how do they match up with what staff members want? I know that I get really excited when we start a new program at school, and I think that everyone will love what I am going to offer. I have found out, however, that people get really excited when you ask them *their* opinion and then develop offerings that *they* are looking for.

For the past three years, I have offered an after-school yoga program. It has been very successful, and the main reason for that success is the teacher, Michele Schulz, who is a certified yoga instructor and the most wonderful teacher you could ever find! She also happens to be the mother of two of my students. What a resource to tap! We have had many staff success stories at our school because of the yoga program, as well as other after-school wellness programs. In the yoga class, I have

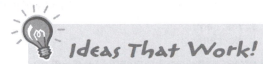

Ideas That Work!

H Tap into the resources that people in your school district have to offer! When you find out what wellness offerings your staff would like to see, put announcements in your school district's newsletter or in the community newspaper that you are looking for someone to teach, for example, yoga. You will be surprised at the resources you find at your fingertips!

been inspired by one of our staff members who came to the first session overweight and had to struggle to use a chair to modify every pose. Now, one year later, she has lost a lot of weight and is dedicated to leading a healthy lifestyle. In yoga, she does every pose with no chair in sight! She motivates me every day with her bright smile and can-do attitude. It does not stop there. For example, two weight loss groups in our school district have lost a total of 600 pounds—wow, that is an impressive number!

Think about what you can do to help jump-start a program at your school. I am sure that there are many wonderful people in your area who would love to be part of a staff wellness program. The best idea we have had at our school was to post a staff wellness survey on the web (see figure 6.1 on page 104). It told us what staff members wanted and got us going in the right direction!

Staff Wellness Action Plan

A great way to put together a step-by-step process for addressing staff wellness is to write an action plan (see figure 6.2 on page 105). The plan provides the mechanism you need in order to record all of the great ideas generated for staff wellness. It can also be used as a checklist for getting each step of the process done. Thus it can serve as an invaluable tool either for starting a new staff wellness program or for improving an existing program!

FIGURE 6.1

Online Staff Wellness Survey

1. I rate my physical fitness as follows:

    a. Excellent
    b. Above average
    c. Average
    d. Poor

2. I am interested in improving both my physical and mental health.

    a. Yes, I am.
    b. No, I am not.

3. I prefer a wellness program that is set up as follows:

    a. Group program
    b. Individual program

4. I would like to have the following areas evaluated:

    a. Weight related to height
    b. Strength
    c. Flexibility
    d. Cardiorespiratory endurance
    e. I do not want to have a fitness evaluation.
    f. Other (specify) _____

5. In a week's time, I usually exercise as follows:

    a. Never
    b. 1 hour every day
    c. 1 hour at least three times a week
    d. 30 minutes every day
    e. 30 minutes at least three times a week
    f. Other (specify) _____

6. The best time for me to participate in a school wellness activity is as follows:

    a. Before school
    b. After school
    c. On the weekends

7. The types of exercise classes that I would like to see offered are as follows (circle all that apply):

    a. Walking program
    b. Yoga
    c. Cardio fitness
    d. Strength training
    e. Other (specify) _____

8. Should time be set aside for family physical fitness events?

    a. Yes
    b. No
    Comments _____

From C. Gorwitz, 2012, *Teaching healthy lifestyles in middle school PE: Strategies from an award-winning program* (Champaign, IL: Human Kinetics).

FIGURE 6.2

Staff Wellness Action Plan

1. List the key people I need to contact in order to improve staff wellness.

_____

_____

_____

2. List the goals of the staff wellness program.

_____

_____

_____

3. List the resources needed in order to be successful (e.g., equipment, wellness books, names of people who can teach classes).

_____

_____

_____

_____

4. Write a step-by-step implementation plan. Here is an example: Step 1—Set up first staff wellness committee meeting.

_____

_____

_____

_____

_____

5. Note other ideas.

_____

_____

_____

_____

Using Pedometers

There are many ways you can use pedometers in working with staff members. First, ask how many of them are willing to wear a pedometer to record the steps they take during the day. Next, contact a company that sells pedometers and see if they are willing to give you a discount if you purchase a large quantity. (Staff members would pay for their own pedometers unless you have funding from another source.) Do not buy cheap pedometers! They will fall apart, and staff members will not be willing to try a new one. I have found that purchasing the middle level of quality usually provides the best balance between cost and durability. Consider what information your participants want to get from the pedometer and keep it simple. You don't need all the bells and whistles offered by top-of-the-line pedometers.

If you need to get funding to pay for the pedometers, you may find that local businesses or nonprofit community groups are a good resource. You can also ask the associations you belong to if they have grant monies available. Grants are sometimes offered on websites. A good place to start your search for funding is your state physical education website. Before contacting a funding source, you must have your plan of action ready to present. Do not just go to a business and ask for pedometers. You must show any potential donor a written plan addressing the goals of the program, how the money will be spent, and how the group's logo will be used in promoting the pedometer program (one approach is to make a poster displaying the names of sponsoring companies and organizations).

One great motivational pedometer activity is a staff challenge that promotes a little fun competition! It also generates interest in the program that will help sustain it over the long run. These are just a few ideas that can get you started:

Ideas That Work!

P Hold healthy staff meetings! Here is a great suggestion to improve the overall health of your staff. Suggest getting rid of the junk food that is typically offered at staff meetings and replace it with healthy offerings! For example, instead of candy, provide pretzels or fresh fruit. At first, people may want to know what happened to their treats, but if you help them consider the fact that there are many different ways to reward oneself other than junk food, they will appreciate it!

- Have teachers at different grade levels challenge each other to see who can get the most steps (e.g., sixth-grade teachers going against seventh-grade teachers).

- Pick a destination that the entire staff can walk to together and have the staff members total their steps and send them to you each week via e-mail.

- Set a weekly goal for steps and use the school's website to highlight the staff member who took the most steps for the week.

Evaluating Fitness Levels

Conduct fitness testing to provide each staff member with baseline information for use in setting goals. Many people are in denial about their weight and current level of fitness. Thus it is crucial to provide accurate testing, along with explanations of why each test is important. Do the testing in a private environment and assure participants that their information will be kept private and stored in a safe place to which only you have access. The results can be used to set individual goals for each staff member to achieve by the end of the program. You can do the same tests again halfway through the program and at the end of the program to track each person's progress or lack thereof and make any needed adjustments, as well as to gain encouragement from success. To explain each test, I would take each test myself to show what it entails! If you do not feel comfortable doing so, you can ask an outside person (e.g., a personal trainer or someone who works in the fitness industry) to demonstrate each test.

At my school, I am fortunate to be able to test our staff's fitness levels by means of fitness testing software (see figure 6.3 for the form I have used). Make sure that you meet with the staff members as a group to explain what each test involves and what the results mean. If you do not provide this

---

FIGURE 6.3

Staff Fitness Testing

Name _____

1. Are you interested in knowing your current fitness level? (Yes/no) _____

2. The following methods of testing are available. Circle the fitness test that you want to do.

   ■ Sit-and-reach (flexibility test)

   ■ Biceps strength (muscular strength test)

   ■ Body mass index (BMI) (height/weight)

3. Are you interested in analyzing your diet? (Yes/no) _____

   If so, you will use the MyPlate website (www.choosemyplate.gov).

From C. Gorwitz, 2012, *Teaching healthy lifestyles in middle school PE: Strategies from an award-winning program* (Champaign, IL: Human Kinetics).

information, you will have a lot of tears flowing when you show the staff members their results. You may face tears anyway, but by providing staff members with all the information beforehand, you enable them to prepare for what you are going to tell them. Make sure to be supportive of each staff member, do follow-ups with them to test their fitness levels and discuss their progress, and give them a lot of encouragement when they start doing their exercise programs after seeing their results.

Individual Workout Programs

Another way in which you can contribute to your colleagues' wellness is to give them basic individual workout programs. (Of course, you should inform them that they need to see their doctor before starting any exercise program.) See figure 6.4 for an example of an exercise program that I would give one of my

---

FIGURE 6.4

Sample Staff Workout Program

Name _____

Remember that you need to see your own doctor before starting an exercise program. Once you are cleared by your doctor, do each one of these days, then repeat. Take the seventh day off as a day of rest!

DAY 1

Warm-Up (10 minutes)

■ Stretch for 10 minutes—exercises will be provided for you by the teacher in charge.

Cardiorespiratory Endurance (20 minutes)

Choose at least one of the following and do it for 20 minutes:

■ Walk on the treadmill.

■ Use the elliptical trainer.

■ Ride the Airdyne bicycle.

■ Walk in the school hallways or outside.

■ Run in the school hallways or outside.

■ Bike outside.

■ Do yoga exercises provided by the instructor.

Muscular Strength Training and Toning (20 minutes)

■ Biceps curls _____ weight used _____ number of reps

■ Overhead curl _____ weight used _____ number of reps

- Triceps (kickbacks) _____ weight used _____ number of reps
- Flys _____ weight used _____ number of reps
- Medicine ball—follow the chart provided by the person in charge.
- Big-ball exercises—follow the chart provided by the person in charge.

DAY 2

Warm-Up (10 minutes)
Stretch for 10 minutes—exercises will be provided by the teacher in charge.

Cardiorespiratory Endurance (20 minutes)
Choose at least one of the following and do it for 20 minutes:

- Walk on the treadmill.
- Use the elliptical trainer.
- Ride the Airdyne bicycle.
- Walk in the school hallways or outside.
- Run in the school hallways or outside.
- Bike outside.
- Do yoga exercises provided by the instructor.

Muscular Strength Training and Toning (20 minutes)
- Biceps curls _____ weight used _____ number of reps
- Overhead curl _____ weight used _____ number of reps
- Triceps (kickbacks) _____ weight used _____ number of reps
- Flys _____ weight used _____ number of reps
- Big-ball exercises—pictures of how to do the exercises will be provided.

DAY 3

Cardiorespiratory Endurance (30 minutes)
Pick a cardiorespiratory endurance activity to do for 30 minutes:

- Walk.
- Run.
- Bike or inline-skate.

Flexibility (30 minutes)
Choose one of the following:

- Perform stretches chosen by the instructor (hold each stretch for a count of 15).
- Do yoga exercises provided to you by the instructor.

From C. Gorwitz, 2012, *Teaching healthy lifestyles in middle school PE: Strategies from an award-winning program* (Champaign, IL: Human Kinetics).

Ideas That Work!

T Laminated lists of healthy websites will help your staff! The web offers a lot of good information that your staff can use. At my school, people are always asking me questions about their health. Most people view you as knowing everything about health, and they want answers from you. Of course, you are not a doctor and cannot diagnose anything, but you can guide the staff in knowing where to go for reliable information. At the beginning of the school year, provide staff members with a card that lists reliable websites for health information. They will really appreciate the list and will know that it is worthwhile because it has come from you! Here are some examples of great websites for reliable health information:

Mayo Clinic (www.mayoclinic.com)
YMCA (www.ymca.net)
U.S. Department of Health and Human Services (www.healthfinder.gov)

staff members. We are fortunate to have an exercise room at my school that includes equipment such as exercise bikes, elliptical machines, big exercise balls, and medicine balls. You can use the workout that I have provided for you as a place to start when providing your staff with an exercise program.

Healthy Group Activities

Start a committee at your school to plan healthy get-togethers throughout the school year. These gatherings need not all be physical—they should also include some time for staff members to relax and recharge their batteries!
    Here are some examples to get you started:

- Take a walk together after school.
- Try out a new exercise program. Many programs will let you try the first session free; examples include yoga studios, YMCAs, and local fitness centers. Contact fitness clubs and ask if they offer a free first visit (let them know that you would have a lot of interested staff members).
- Find out the interests of the group and which staff members have expertise in a chosen area, then set up a time to try it out. For example, if someone at your school is great at jewelry making, arrange a get-together to make something. If a staff member enjoys cooking and is willing to help, invite the group to get together and make healthy snacks!
- Go enjoy a free concert in the park.
- Go to a nature preserve and enjoy a scenic walk.
- Meet at a pool and take a dip!
- Get a pedicure or manicure together!
- Meet at a bookstore and walk around while talking about books that participants have enjoyed!

Summary

A good staff wellness program can help change the whole climate of a school. When people feel good about themselves, they are much more productive! Participating in activities outside of the school building can also bring people closer together. Staff members can identify colleagues who have common interests and thus enjoy a chance to share ideas. Making wellness a priority can also reduce the number of sick days that employees take. Staff wellness is a winning idea for any school to undertake!

Challenge Questions

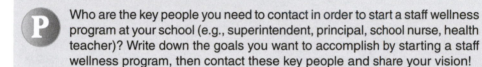

P Who are the key people you need to contact in order to start a staff wellness program at your school (e.g., superintendent, principal, school nurse, health teacher)? Write down the goals you want to accomplish by starting a staff wellness program, then contact these key people and share your vision!

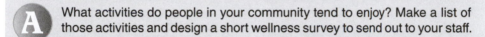

A What activities do people in your community tend to enjoy? Make a list of those activities and design a short wellness survey to send out to your staff.

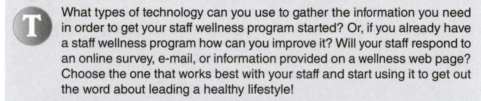

T What types of technology can you use to gather the information you need in order to get your staff wellness program started? Or, if you already have a staff wellness program how can you improve it? Will your staff respond to an online survey, e-mail, or information provided on a wellness web page? Choose the one that works best with your staff and start using it to get out the word about leading a healthy lifestyle!

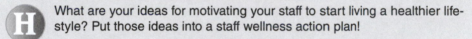

H What are your ideas for motivating your staff to start living a healthier lifestyle? Put those ideas into a staff wellness action plan!

After-School and Summer Programs

Promote a healthy lifestyle beyond the classroom!

You stress leading a healthy lifestyle to all of your classes, but do you want that message to be emphasized only during the school day? No! You want your students to take all of that great information with them in their "healthy lifestyle backpack," along with their skills in math, reading, and science! You can help kids apply what they're learning in your class to their lives away from school by setting up after-school and summer programs.

Approach the PATH . . .

With obesity on the rise, students need healthy lifestyle education not only in physical education class but also in an after-school or summer program. When you are **planning** such programs, consider the following steps.

1. Write down one or two achievable healthy lifestyle goals you want students to reach through your programs.

2. Construct a program budget. If funds are lacking, do not let that discourage you! Many grants are available to help schools start an after-school or summer program or enrich an existing program.

3. Create a list of the healthy lifestyle ideas you want to include in your program.

In this chapter, I share with you examples of many ready-made healthy lifestyle activities that will help you start on the path to a successful after-school or summer program!

What are the favorite **activities** among kids and their families in your area? How can you include these activities in your after-school and summer programs? Offer activities that will excite the members of your school community! Do your students spend the summer inside playing video games? You can motivate them to move by providing them with an individualized Sunshine Calendar (instructions are provided in this chapter) to inspire them during the summer months.

Use your teacher website to promote your after-school or summer program ideas! Ask your **technology** director if a link can be placed on your school's main web page to direct students, their families, and community members to your page of information about after-school and summer programs. You can also use technology to create a checkout system (described in this chapter) through which students and their families can borrow pedometers and heart rate monitors for after-school use.

Look to work in **harmony** with local businesses by forming partnerships that help you promote healthy lifestyles in your community. Creating a community awareness program with local businesses will spark interest in living a healthy lifestyle. Local businesses (e.g., a health club or organic grocery store) can often provide you with ideas and funding for your program!

After-School Programs

The after-school programs that I have been part of have been short-term programs that I started with an emphasis on the specific interests of my students. In doing these programs, I have started small and addressed the needs of my students. To decide what after-school programs would work in your school, assess your students' needs, as well as the resources available to you (e.g., time, facilities, staff, volunteers).

You should also consider what specific talents and passions you can bring to the program. Are you an avid runner who would like to start a running program? Do you like to kayak or bike, and do you have access to equipment and an area at your school to conduct such programs? Take a minute to think about your school and the interests that both you and your students have. Then jot down your ideas.

The following sections of this chapter describe program ideas that I have used with the middle school students at my school. They all started out with ideas that either my students or I brought up during class. By reading about these ideas, you can find at least one that will work at your school— or that sparks an idea of your own to start using at your school!

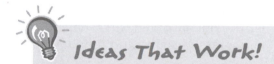

Ideas That Work!

P Incorporate the interests of your students into an after-school program. What do students in your area like to do? What activities could you offer that would interest your students? Survey your students about what their families like to do for exercise as a family! You will then be able to provide your students with information in your classes about the specific areas of interest that they indicated in the survey.

Library Pedometer Checkout

Once I began using pedometers in my physical education classes, students would ask me if they could wear the pedometers outside of class to see how many steps they were taking in other parts of the day. I told them that I was excited by the idea but did not have any extra pedometers to give them. However, instead of letting it drop there, I looked around and found a grant that could be used to buy the extra pedometers (my state physical education association provides grants to member teachers)! In fact, most of the projects I have done have been funded by a grant. If you have an idea but no money, don't let that discourage you! Plenty of grants are out there to help fund your ideas. State physical education associations may offer grants and other funding resources that can help you fund a creative project. I have received several small grants from my state association, and they have really helped jump-start my program! Contact your state president and ask about the funding resources offered by your state association.

Another possible funding resource is our national physical education association: AAHPERD (American Alliance for Health, Physical Education, Recreation and Dance). Go to the AAHPERD website (www.aahperd.org) and explore the current funding options. For example, I wanted to start an after-school running club, and, in connection with AAHPERD, the ING corporation offered a running grant that I won 2 years in a row. Most of the grant applications are easy to fill out, and they can help you find the funds needed to get started.

Local businesses in your area are also a great funding resource. Contact a local business and set up a meeting to describe your plan of action and how you will showcase the local business during the after-school activities.

It is also worth checking with your own school's technology department regarding funding for heart rate monitors, pedometers, and other types of technology that you want to include in your program. Set up a meeting with your technology director and describe your plan and the funding it needs in order to be successful.

Finally, the web serves as a great way to look for funding sources. Just use your favorite search engine and key words (e.g., healthy after-school program ideas) to find funding resources in your area. These are just a few of the options out there for funding. Let your imagination take flight and find funding for the great ideas that you have!

So, we now have 30 pedometers available in our school library for students to check out. A library aide came up with the idea of putting a library barcode on each pedometer to facilitate the checkout process. Students can check out a pedometer for 2 weeks. They can even check out one for each family member!

Ideas That Work!

H Use a library pedometer checkout system to get families exercising together! By allowing students to check out pedometers for each family member, you provide an opportunity for families to move together. Word spreads pretty fast, and soon you'll have a lot of families exercising together!

Pedometers are stored in a box with numbered dividers to make organization easy.

I also include a mileage sheet (1 mile = 2,000 steps) in the pedometer checkout to encourage exercising outside of school. You could even have the students turn in their mileage sheets for extra credit. It's also a good idea to provide information about community walking resources—for example, your park district might publish a map of local trails that you can distribute. Finally, consider providing the pedometer, mileage sheet, and walking resources together in a plastic bag at the checkout for convenience.

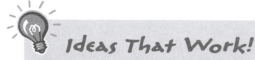

Ideas That Work!

H Local businesses are a great resource to tap into for help with purchasing equipment for checkout! Think of the local businesses in your area and make a list of the ones you think might be willing either to donate equipment or to give you money to help you start the program. You could offer to put up a sign at the checkout station or in the front entrance to your school featuring the name of the business! What other ideas do you have for involving local businesses? Jot down a list of ideas for making your desired program a reality.

I encourage students and their families to use the pedometers to estimate mileage when they walk local trails or courses. Once the student or family member has used the pedometer and calculated the mileage—we use 2,000 steps as the equivalent of 1 mile (1.6 km)—they can then track their mileage when using those trails without a pedometer.

I have also suggested some specific challenges to get students and their families started! Here are a few ideas I've used:

- Ask students how many different trails they can walk in a (specified time frame).
- Challenge students to try to take at least 10,000 steps every day!
- Create a trail around your school and make a map of it, including how many steps you took in following it. Then include a copy of the map with each pedometer at checkout.
- Destination challenges: It's always fun to inform the students how many steps it would take to walk to a certain destination (e.g., a national park or a favorite summer destination like Washington D.C.) and then have students accumulate that number of steps.

Jog Your Mind With Reading

This 6-week after-school program that combined reading and running was very successful! Students met twice a week with a language arts teacher and did a lot of reading and writing activities. They also met twice a week with me and another language arts teacher (who is a runner) and did running, walking, and other exercise activities. It was great working with these two teachers who had wonderful ideas for activities that we could do.

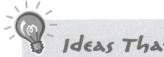

Ideas That Work!

H Survey your staff to find volunteers who would do reading and running activities! I am sure there are many people on your staff who would love to be part of this program. Set up a sign-up sheet by your teacher mailboxes and ask willing teachers to volunteer to help! Check with your principal for course approval, facility scheduling, and so on beforehand.

Divide the class into two groups and have them take turns participating in reading activities and in running and other exercise activities. The sky is the limit for what you can include in this program. Before the program starts, meet with the teachers involved and plan out all the activities. Ask the other teacher volunteers for ideas about what to include in the program. Here are some ideas for reading and writing activities:

- Students read poetry and create their own poems about wellness.
- Teacher or leader reads a picture book with a wellness theme, and students then create their own short stories about their favorite activities.
- Students journal about their feelings when they are participating in their favorite activity.

Here are some ideas for running activities:

- Clothespin run: Create a running course. Each time the student completes a lap, he or she receives a clothespin (or other object).
- Animal relay race: Set up a running course, have the kids get into groups of four, and have each group's members spread out around the course. Hand the first person in the group a beanbag animal (e.g., frog, turtle, gorilla). That person starts running while holding the beanbag animal. Upon getting to the second person, the runner hands off the beanbag animal, and this continues until all four people have received the animal and run with it.
- Pedometer step race: Designate a length of time (let's say 15 minutes) and have the kids run or walk for the duration. The goal is to see who can accumulate the most steps during that time.

We created a checkoff sheet to help students monitor their accomplishments in this program (see figure 7.1). Each box represents one session of running or reading in which the student participated. The student checks off one box for each day in which they finish the indicated activity. The goal is to check off all of the boxes on the sheet.

At the end of this program, we had a healthy snack party! Before the party, we got the whole group together and held a discussion about examples of healthy snacks. After the discussion, everyone was assigned a healthy snack to bring to the party. What would you and your students like to do to culminate your reading and jogging group?

FIGURE 7.1

Jog Your Mind With Reading

| Read after school with your reading teacher. | Exercise after school with your PE teacher and language arts teacher. | Read after school with your reading teacher. | Exercise after school with your PE teacher and language arts teacher. | Read after school with your reading teacher. |

Exercise after school with your PE teacher and language arts teacher.

Read after school with your reading teacher.

Read after school with your reading teacher.

Exercise after school with your PE teacher and language arts teacher.

Other Ideas

Here are a few more ideas for after-school activities:

- **Twister Fitness Game.** Have your students design a Twister-style spinner card featuring the following terms: cardiorespiratory endurance, muscular strength, muscular endurance, flexibility, and body composition and nutrition. Use colored tape to make circles on the floor. Each circle should contain a written example of one of the categories shown on the spinner card, such as doing biceps curls with weights (muscular endurance) or eating a salad for lunch (body composition and nutrition). Students spin the spinner and call out the indicated category when the spinner's arrow stops. The student doing the contortions puts his or her foot or hand on the colored circle containing an example that corresponds with the category indicated by the spinner!

- **Weighted Hula Hoops.** Using large weighted hoops, have your students hula-hoop to music. If you put on dance music, the kids can try to hula-hoop and perform dance moves at the same time.

- **Water Bottle Weights.** Have your students put sand into empty water bottles to create weights that they can use in performing various fitness activities. Provide stickers and decorative tape for the kids to use in personalizing their water bottles.

Summer Programs

Long days, no school, and lots of sunshine. . . . There's no better time than summer for a kid to be active! And there's no reason why your students should just sit inside and watch TV or play video games when there are so many opportunities to get outside and move. A lot of kids have no idea how much better they'd feel and how much they'd enjoy themselves if they just took that first step outside! As their teacher, you can provide the motivation and guidance they need.

My students also have the option of completing the Sunshine Fitness Calendar (see figure 7.2) while they're on summer break. This calendar lists suggested categories of activity and students use the calendar and categories to plan out their own activities in class before summer starts. They should plan for each day of the week and can use the calendar to remind

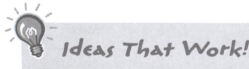

Ideas That Work!

H Provide times outside of the school day when students can show their families what they are doing in physical education class to promote a healthy lifestyle! Find a space that you can reserve at your school for students to bring in their family members to learn about healthy living. If your school has a gymnasium, you could reserve it on a Sunday night and have equipment available for your students to use in showing their families ways to lead an actively healthy life.

FIGURE 7.2

Sunshine Fitness Calendar

Body composition and nutrition	Cardiorespiratory endurance	Muscular strength, muscular endurance, and flexibility	Cardiorespiratory endurance	Muscular strength, muscular endurance, and flexibility	Cardiorespiratory endurance	Rest
			1	2	3	4
5 Healthy eating weekly goal: Eat strawberries this week!	6 Walk my dogs for 30 minutes today!	7 Do 10 push-ups, 10 sit-ups, and 5 yoga poses when I get out of bed today!	8 Run around the block two times!	9 Use weighted water bottles to do 10 biceps curls. Do my favorite leg stretch and hold it for 30 seconds.	10 Jump rope 50 times forward and 50 times backward.	11 Rest and read a good book!
12 Healthy eating weekly goal: No energy drinks this week!	13	14	15	16	17	18
19 Healthy eating weekly goal:	20	21	22	23	24	25
26 Healthy eating weekly goal:	27	28	29	30	Notes:	

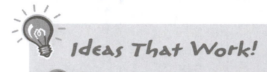

Ideas That Work!

P Starting with written objectives helps you attain your goal. By starting with your objectives, you develop a clear-cut goal to shoot for when doing this project! Make sure that your objectives are attainable for your students and your program. In this chapter, I provide you with ideas that I have successfully used in my physical education program, and you can build your own ideas from there!

themselves of the principles of fitness (e.g., cardiorespiratory endurance, muscular strength, muscular endurance, flexibility, and body composition and nutrition) that they've learned all year long. It encourages them to pursue a healthy lifestyle on their own time—not just in PE class! And it can be used as a great goal-setting tool. I love this project because it wraps up all of the concepts that I have covered during the school year. The five components of fitness are emphasized along with healthy eating.

I have found that kids really like incentives for accomplishing their goals during the summer. Choose incentives that are the right fit for your students. The incentive for my students is that when they turn in their completed Sunshine Fitness Calendar, they receive time off of their first heart rate monitor workout.

Creating the Calendar

Your Sunshine Fitness Calendar should pull together everything that you have taught throughout the school year about the five components of fitness: cardiorespiratory endurance, muscular strength, muscular endurance, flexibility, and body composition and nutrition. What a great way not only to talk about the importance of these fitness components but also to help students put them into practice in their lives outside of school.

I label two columns on the calendar as muscular strength, muscular endurance, and flexibility columns and three others as cardiorespiratory endurance columns. I have found that this approach gives students a good visual of how often they need to include these components in their workouts. I stress the importance of getting 60 minutes of daily exercise but have found that giving students a visual labeled at the top of each column helps them to fill out the calendar correctly. When you introduce the calendar to your students, discuss the importance of getting 60 minutes of exercise each day. Then, while the students are filling out the calendars in class, you can walk around and make sure that each student includes the correct amount of exercise time! Have the kids list the specific amount of time that they are going to spend on each activity they list on the calendar and check that every day includes at least 60 minutes.

I also strongly recommend that you devote one column on your calendar to body composition and nutrition. Students can choose one healthy food to try for a week—or one junk food item to give up for that week! (I also include energy drinks in my discussion because a lot of my students are drinking more than three of these a day!) You have been talking all school year about healthy eating, and now your students can put all of that information to use in their plan for the summer!

Filling out this calendar creates a lot of teachable moments for discussing healthy food versus junk food. Even though you have been discussing this distinction throughout the school year, there will still be kids who want to challenge you about eating junk food!

I have given much thought to the question of how to integrate technology into this project. I have yet to implement the following ideas but want to put them out there for you to consider. Maybe they will spark ideas for you!

> ### Ideas That Work!
>
> **T** Go paperless for the environment! Instead of handing out a paper calendar to all students, consider putting a blank calendar (including ideas for activities) on your physical education web page and encouraging students to copy or download it to their own computer.

- Make pedometers and heart rate monitors available for checkout during the summer months. Students can then record their heart rates and step counts on their summer calendar.
- List healthy eating websites on the calendar stored on your physical education website. Students can check out the websites on their own time and find great information about healthy eating.
- List websites offering healthy recipes that students can use to make simple healthy snacks on their own during the summer.

Lesson Progression

The following teaching progression outlines in step-by-step fashion how I teach the Sunshine Fitness Calendar in my classes. I build into my teaching calendar an assumption of 2 days of inclement weather that we use to stay inside and complete this project. The project has made a difference in my students' lives. Read over the following description of how I have taught this lesson, then shape it into the lesson that you would like to teach!

DAY 1

Before Class Starts

- Prepare the space for the Word Wall Fitness activity (see chapter 4, page 62, for a description). You need enough paper for all classes.
- Set out pedometers for students to put on.
- Post five pieces of tagboard on the wall—one for each of the components of fitness: cardiorespiratory endurance, muscular strength, muscular endurance, flexibility, and body composition and nutrition. Place a marker at each piece of tagboard. (Write the class name and hour on each piece of tagboard and write "Next Class" on the back so that the students can use the piece for activities on day 2.)
- Set up a music player.
- Set up a projector with which to show students your completed calendar.
- Arrange the needed equipment for the Word Wall Fitness activity and for the fitness breaks during the lesson (you should have exercise balls, steppers, jump ropes [short and long], hand weights, footballs, and flying discs). You need enough equipment so that every student has something to use without having to share.

Start class with the Word Wall Fitness activity. You need to have a different concept to use for each class so that the first-hour students do not give it away to students in the next hour's class. During the activity, discuss with your students what constitutes a healthy lifestyle for people their age (stress the importance of getting 60 minutes of exercise each day and taking 10,000 steps daily).

Ideas That Work!

T Design a simple web page for your physical education program! This is a great way to provide all sorts of information to your students, staff members, and even community members. You do not have to have an elaborate web page. You can start out small and include your grading policy, the units that you teach, and a discussion of exercise options for families and students.

After the activity, take a 5-minute exercise break. Remind the students of the importance of getting 60 minutes of exercise and taking 10,000 steps each day. Tell them that they have 5 minutes to find a piece of equipment and do as many steps or as much exercise as they can.

Following the exercise break, explain the Sunshine Fitness Calendar. Use a projector to show the class a finished example of the calendar. Explain to the students that they will fill out their own calendar for the summer with exercises that they can do outside of class. Again (yes, again!), emphasize 60 minutes of exercise and 10,000 steps a day.

Assign your students into five numbered groups and assign each number to a piece of tagboard. Each piece of tagboard lists a component of fitness (cardiorespiratory endurance, muscular strength, muscular endurance, flexibility, or body composition and nutrition). Start your music and have students work together to generate ideas for each component of fitness that they could use in filling out their summer calendar. At your signal, the groups rotate from one tagboard to the next until each group has visited all five tagboards and written down their ideas. For the body composition and nutrition board, they write down nutritious foods or give examples of alternatives to fast food.

Gather the groups together and move as a class from one tagboard to the next while reviewing what the students have written down. Ask everyone in class to make suggestions. When class ends, remind the students yet again of the importance of 60 minutes of exercise and 10,000 steps. Tell them that on the next class day they will fill out their own calendars.

Take all of the classes' tagboards and type up a separate sheet for each of the five components (cardiorespiratory endurance and so on) listing the examples that the classes came up with. Share the sheets with the students on the next class day.

DAY 2

Before Class Starts

- Type up all of the exercise examples that the students wrote on the five tagboards the previous day and post them around the gym. Take each class around the gym and read the examples from each sheet of tagboard (e.g., cardiorespiratory endurance: jumping rope, walking the dog, jogging, riding a bike).
- Set up your music player.
- Gather students' fitness testing information and personal goal sheets (see chapter 2).
- Bring blank calendars (one for each student).
- Set up the needed equipment in the middle of the floor for the exercise breaks.

To start class, do the Clip-On Composition activity (see chapter 4, page 73). After the warm-up, distribute and review the students' fitness test results and goal sheets. Emphasize that if a student's score is not where he or she would like it to be, the student should concentrate on doing exercises during the summer to help him or her improve in that area. Student who have met all of their goals should set higher goals to achieve during the next year and plan to do exercises during the summer to help them prepare to achieve their new goals.

Next, divide the class into five groups and hand out the blank calendars. Explain that the students should each fill out a calendar listing exercises that they will actually do during the summer. They should also list nutritious food that they will eat. Each group starts at a different tagboard (cardiorespiratory endurance, muscular strength, muscular endurance, flexibility, or body composition and nutrition) and begins to fill out their calendars. In the nutrition box, they write a nutritious food that they will eat that week or list an alternative to eat instead of fast food. Play music while the students work; at appropriate time intervals, stop the music to prompt the students to move to the next piece of tagboard.

After the students have done two stations, give them a 5- to 8-minute exercise break and tell them to use the equipment in the middle. Emphasize that each student should have his or her own piece of equipment and should be moving! They can use the long jump ropes as a group.

After the exercise break, have the students do the last three stations. Make sure that they list a nutritious food or fast food alternative in each of the four nutrition boxes.

Inform the students that you will return their calendars after grading them according to the rubric (see figure 7.3 on page 126) and that they will then take them home for use during the summer. If the students bring them back completed and signed by their parents in the fall, they will receive a reward (e.g., time off during their first heart rate monitor workout done in the fall).

Assessment

Make sure that your students always know exactly how they will be assessed for everything you grade. In this case, show your students an example of a correctly done calendar from the past year, then show them the rubric you will use for grading their calendars. You can use my rubric (see figure 7.3) as it appears or make changes to fit the calendar project as you will be using it!

FIGURE 7.3

Sunshine Fitness Calendar Rubric

Name _____

Description	6	4	1	
Cardiorespiratory endurance: 60 minutes of exercise on 5 days a week for 4 weeks	60 minutes of exercise on 5 days a week for 4 weeks	60 minutes of exercise on 4 days a week	60 minutes of exercise on 3 days a week or fewer	
Muscular strength and muscular endurance: Strength workout on 2 days a week for 4 weeks	Strength workout on 2 days a week for 4 weeks	Strength workout on 2 days a week for 3 weeks	Strength workout on 2 days a week for 2 weeks or fewer	
Flexibility: 2 stretches at the end of 2 workouts a week for 4 weeks	2 stretches at the end of 2 workouts a week for 4 weeks	2 stretches at the end of 2 workouts a week for 3 weeks	2 stretches at the end of 2 workouts a week for 2 weeks	
Body composition and nutrition: Nutrition block filled in with nutritious food eaten or alternative for fast food	Nutrition block lists nutritious food eaten or junk food or soda replaced by alternative for 4 weeks	Nutrition block lists nutritious food eaten or junk food or soda replaced by alternative for 3 weeks	Nutrition block lists nutritious food eaten or junk food or soda replaced by alternative for 2 weeks	
			TOTAL	

Summary

You can help improve the lives of your students and others in the community by developing programs that help your students live a healthy lifestyle when they're not at school! By incorporating the activities presented in this chapter, you can help your students be more active in their everyday lives. Including local businesses in your program not only provides a funding resource but also helps motivate other members of your community to become more active! The more opportunities your students and their families have to participate in healthy lifestyle activities, the more likely they are to choose not only to exercise but also to incorporate healthy eating into their lives.

Challenge Questions

P What is the goal of your after-school program for healthy living? What steps can you take to start or improve it? Name one local business that might provide funding or other assistance in planning your after-school program.

A What types of activity do you want to include in your after-school program? How can you use the Sunshine Fitness Calendar activity at your school? What types of equipment will you need to start or improve your after-school program?

T How could you use your teacher web page to promote wellness outside of the school? Do you have access to pedometers, heart rate monitors, or other types of technology for use in your after-school program? Describe your plan to integrate technology into your after-school program.

H What teachers at your school can help you start a reading and exercise program? Who at your school can help you implement an after-school healthy lifestyle program? (List specific names.) What local businesses can you contact for funding and support?

Index

Note: The letters *f* and *t* after page numbers indicate figures and tables, respectively.

About the Author

Crystal Gorwitz has been teaching physical education since 1992. She is a 2001 Carol M. White PEP grant recipient, the 2003 Wisconsin Middle School Physical Education Teacher of the Year, the 2003 Midwest Middle School Teacher of the Year, and the 2004 NASPE National Middle School Physical Education Teacher of the Year. She also was selected for the 2011 Champion Award from the Alliance for a Healthier Generation.

A teacher at Hortonville Middle School in Hortonville, Wisconsin, Gorwitz led her school in receiving NASPE STARS School Awards in 2005 and 2008. This award recognizes schools with physical education programs of excellence. Under her guidance, her school also received a Bronze Award from the Alliance for a Healthy Generation, which recognizes schools that provide a healthy environment for students' learning.

Gorwitz is a member of the American Alliance for Health, Physical Education, Recreation and Dance (AAHPERD) and is president-elect of Wisconsin AHPERD. In her spare time, she enjoys doing yoga, fishing, and kayaking.

You'll find other outstanding physical education resources at
www.HumanKinetics.com

In the U.S. call 1.800.747.4457
Australia 08 8372 0999
Canada. 1.800.465.7301
Europe . . . . .+44 (0) 113 255 5665
New Zealand . . . 0064 9 448 1207

HUMAN KINETICS
The Information Leader in Physical Activity
P.O. Box 5076 • Champaign, IL 61825-5076